PENGUIN BOOKS

LEADERSHIP AND
THE WHIRLPOOL EFFECT™

Lester Levy was born and educated in South Africa, where he graduated with a degree in medicine. Arriving in New Zealand in 1978 he altered his direction to take up a career in business, graduating with a Masters of Business Administration. His formative management career was with major multinational companies. Following a secondment to the Department of the Prime Minister and Cabinet, he took the position as chief executive of South Auckland Health, one of the largest public health providers in New Zealand. Lester has twice been awarded the prestigious Kings Fund International Fellowship from the Kings Fund in London. He is now managing director of a health sector investment bank. Lester also sits on a number of boards, as a director and chairman, in both New Zealand and Australia.

Lester is married to Debbie, and they live with their children Samuel and Madison in St Heliers, Auckland.

This book is dedicated to Debbie, my wife,
and also my children
Darren, Samuel and Madison

LEADERSHIP and THE WHIRLPOOL EFFECT™

Why New Zealand managers
are failing to deliver to their
potential — and what can
be done about it

Lester Levy

http://www.whirlpooleffect.co.nz

PENGUIN BOOKS

PENGUIN BOOKS

Penguin Books (NZ) Ltd, cnr Airborne and Rosedale Roads, Albany,
Auckland 1310, New Zealand
Penguin Books Ltd, 27 Wrights Lane, London W8 5TZ, England
Penguin USA, 375 Hudson Street, New York, NY 10014, United States
Penguin Books Australia Ltd, 487 Maroondah Highway, Ringwood,
Australia 3134
Penguin Books Canada Ltd, 10 Alcorn Avenue, Toronto, Ontario, Canada M4V 3B2
Penguin Books (South Africa) Pty Ltd, 4 Pallinghurst Road, Parktown,
Johannesburg 2193, South Africa

Penguin Books Ltd, Registered Offices: Harmondsworth, Middlesex, England

First published by Penguin Books (NZ) Ltd, 1999

1 3 5 7 9 10 8 6 4 2

Copyright © Lester Levy, 1999

The right of Lester Levy to be identified as the author of this work in terms of
section 96 of the Copyright Act 1994 is hereby asserted.

Editorial services by Michael Gifkins & Associates
Cartoons by Malcolm Walker
Designed by Mary Egan
Typeset by Egan-Reid Ltd
Printed in Australia by Australian Print Group, Maryborough

CONTENTS

http://www.whirlpooleffect.co.nz

FOREWORD

Lester Levy first came to the attention of New Zealanders as the young and progressive chief executive of South Auckland Health. He was a leader that operated in the turbulent climate of national health reforms, but somehow was able to inspire his organisation to achieve positive results at a time when many other organisations were floundering.

Lester seemed to know something about 'managing' that others appeared to have missed.

After reading about Lester Levy, I was delighted to meet him four years ago in 1994. The two of us were asked to assist with Professor Bob Elliott's Diatranz programme, which offers a potential cure to the growing numbers of diabetics in the world. Over the last four years I have grown to admire Lester as a wonderful communicator and a person who is able to get the best out of people through collaboration and highlighting positives.

I have learnt myself — through starting an organisation from scratch 16 years ago that today employs 5,000 people with a market Cap exceeding $700m — that leadership, not management, is the key to inspiring and motivating people. Our organisation, The Warehouse, has grown through our ability to 'put people first' and to strive to get the right balance between our five stakeholders: customers, team members, suppliers, shareholders and the community. If people feel empowered rather than simply delegated to, if they have a sense of true ownership in the organisation in which they spend the majority of their daily lives, then they too crave for the same success factor as do the management and the shareholders.

Lester Levy's management style is worth watching out for and learning from. It is totally consistent with ours at The Warehouse and in both cases this style has proved to be highly successful.

I am personally a great believer in putting the interests of your stakeholders before self interest and therefore fully subscribe to Lester's view. Leadership incorporates listening to the other members of your team, continuing to raise the bar, employing technology that adds value not cost, and putting total trust in your team. Lester has demonstrated these unique qualities and I believe that if more business people follow this lead success will follow.

Stephen Tindall ONZM
Managing Director
The Warehouse Group Ltd

AUTHOR'S NOTE

Leadership and the Whirlpool Effect™ has been primarily written for people in management or leadership positions at any level, whether it be the private or public sector, central or local government, profit or not-for-profit organisations. However, its application extends to all that bear the consequences of management decisions — employees, trade unions and in particular customers. If this book serves to stimulate more people involved in management and those affected by their decisions to think more deeply about the concept of leadership, then it will have served its purpose.

The publication of *Leadership and the Whirlpool Effect*™ is the first and exclusive release of The Whirlpool Effect™ model. The model and the advice and experiences I share in this book have developed as a result of my deep interest in organisations and companies reaching their potential. However, many are in a perilous situation of possible danger and collapse. Leadership not management is what will save these ailing organisations and companies. The Whirlpool Effect™, appropriately used, can assist in identifying where the current defects are, highlighting dangers and indicating urgency.

The Whirlpool Effect™ model is not in itself a simple answer to a complex problem. However, I believe, it does have a practical role to play. More than that, The Whirlpool Effect™ model and the approach taken in this book seek to promote and provoke debate, discussion and, yes, even argument about how our organisations and companies should be led and managed.

I expect and welcome criticism. It is an openness to challenge that creates the opportunity for all of us involved in the world of management to improve and better shape our perspectives.

I have enjoyed reading about management and leadership and have been influenced by the work of Peter Drucker, Ken Blanchard, David Ulrich, Douglas Smith, Stephen Covey, James Heskett, Neil Snyder, James Dowd Jr, Dianne Houghton, David Ogilvy, Amanda Sinclair, Patrick Townsend, Joan Gebhardt, Leonard Schlesinger, Michel Robert, Gary Hamel, C.K. Prahalad, John Wareham, James Donnely Jr, James Kouzes, Barry Posner, Michael Hammer, James Champy, John Kotter, Craig Hickman, Henry Mintzberg, Abraham Zaleznik, Charles Handy and Peter Senge. They have helped enrich my understanding especially when their ideas and concepts have been reinforced by my own practical experience.

I have been privileged to work with a number of interesting and successful people, from whom I have learned enduring lessons, many of which emerge in some shape or form in the book. It is not possible to mention everyone individually, but I would like to take the opportunity to acknowledge Brian Henschall, Nick Marsh, Wayne Cartwright, Robin Milne and Brian Lewis as individuals who helped me develop a deeper curiosity about human interaction and organisational development.

I also acknowledge Terry Harris, from whom I learnt the value of perseverance, patience and consistency; Ross Keenan for his commercial mentorship; Noel Robinson for encouraging my entrepreneurial tendencies; John Scott for his wisdom and ethical approach; Dave Clarke and Harley Gray for their support through challenging times.

I would like to mention Mike Hutcheson, who has an intriguing way of describing human interaction, and Jim Hopkins, an exceptional speaker. I have adapted one of his stories for this book. I would also like to acknowledge my close friend Paul Holmes; he has an instinctive understanding of human behaviour that has helped focus some of my perspectives.

The book would not have been possible without the support, professionalism and enthusiasm of Geoff Walker and Nicola Strawbridge at Penguin Books. I am grateful to Susannah Young for her assistance with both the diagrams and the wordprocessing. Thanks also to Stephen Tindall for writing the foreword. Stephen is an exceptional businessman and leader and I value his support. Finally, I thank my parents, their self-sacrifice to encourage my own education has always been, and will always be, greatly appreciated.

PART 1

THE WHIRLPOOL EFFECT™

ONE

THE PLACID WATER IS
THE PLACE TO BE

Society is always taken by surprise at any
new example of common sense.

— Ralph Waldo Emerson

A gleaming dark blue late model European saloon entered the airport valet carpark. The driver, a confident, dark-haired man in his early forties, adjusted the rear-view mirror slightly, to allow him the opportunity to check his hair as he pulled into his allocated carpark.

Satisfied with his appearance, he reset the mirror, leaned over to the back seat and retrieved his briefcase and coat. He walked purposefully into the airline building towards the business class check-in counter. Once checked in he headed to the club lounge, and following a number of brief conversations with various business acquaintances, he selected a seat next to a large window.

He set down his coat and satchel and approached the breakfast buffet where he selected yoghurt, a croissant, butter, jam and a black coffee. He returned to his seat and started to eat his breakfast. He reached for his cellphone in his inside suit jacket pocket, called his secretary, providing her with a number of crisp instructions. When he finished the call he returned the cellphone to his pocket, took a bound report from his satchel and settled down to read it. He particularly seemed interested in two pages filled with columns and rows of numbers.

This is an image of a man in control . . . a manager in charge.

The swimmer surfaced after yet another dive and became anxious when he realised that the landmarks had altered. The current had obviously taken him downstream much further than he had anticipated. Both riverbanks were at challenging distances. Confident in his swimming ability, he started to swim slightly downstream and towards the left bank.

His strategy was that the mounting current and his own propulsion would work in concert to bring him safely to the left riverbank. As he swam he struggled increasingly with the current, which appeared to get stronger and stronger. Despite his best endeavours the current was forcing him downstream, slowly at first and then quite rapidly.

He started to panic as he realised the water was now in control and he was powerless to overcome its mounting strength. The current had reached such a velocity that it was almost catapulting him forward. Panic overcame him as he heard the eerie sound of his ultimate fate . . . he was being dragged mercilessly towards a whirlpool. Within seconds he was being thrashed around by the force of the whirlpool before being sucked into its vortex.

This is an image of a man in danger . . . a manager being consigned to his fate.

What possible relevance do these vastly different situations have to management today?

They may not be as different as they initially appear. It

is clear to both the swimmer and to any observer of his predicament, that upon surfacing from the dive he was at risk. Recognising this risk, he attempted to reach the safety of the riverbank, but had underestimated the force of the current and was eventually rendered powerless. His fate was no longer under his control.

At first sight the manager at the airport appears safe and in control. There are no visible signs of danger either to him or to an observer. However, without realising it, he may be like the swimmer surfacing from the dive. He may not yet have realised that the landmarks have changed and that the current has taken him further downstream than he had anticipated. He may even be hurtling unknowingly towards a whirlpool, his fate like that of the swimmer, no longer under his control.

Where there is a significant difference between these two scenarios is that the swimmer by his own actions has put himself, and himself only, at risk. The manager puts not only himself, but his employees, his creditors, his company and possibly his community at risk.

This example is by way of introduction to a new management concept that I call The Whirlpool Effect™. The centre of a naturally occurring whirlpool is like a tornado in water, an extremely powerful and destructive force with a strong downward drag. Surrounding the centre of the whirlpool is an area of water with rough concentric currents, much like extremely strong gales. Anything that reaches this area of water will almost inevitably be sucked down into the vortex of the whirlpool.

The area of water adjacent to this has strong and forceful currents analogous to strong winds with unpredictable, powerful gusts. Anything in this area of water is at risk, if exposed to such a gust it may be in danger of being pulled into the adjacent, much more dangerous, gale-force area.

The body of water adjacent to this has a general current

directed towards the centre of the whirlpool but which becomes less powerful as you move further from the vortex. These currents are more like mild to moderate winds within the water.

Surrounding this area is placid water with no current at all. Anything here is relatively safe from the insidious physical pull of the whirlpool.

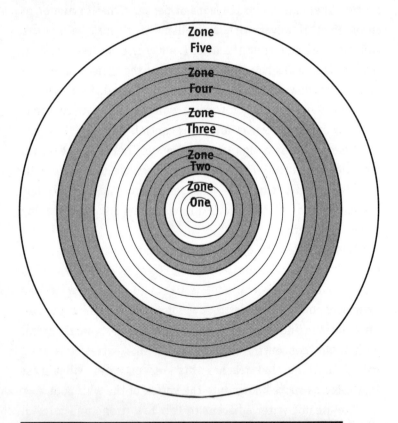

KEY:	
Zone One:	*Tornado*
Zone Two:	*Powerful Gale*
Zone Three:	*Strong Winds with Unpredictably Powerful Gusts*
Zone Four:	*Mild to Moderate Winds*
Zone Five:	*Placid*

From a management perspective The Whirlpool Effect™ describes a phenomenon that is both invisible and intangible. There is a force that draws managers and their organisations towards the centre of the whirlpool, much like gravity exerts a physical pull towards the centre of the earth. My underlying thesis is that this force is ceaselessly present and managers and their organisations are constantly at risk of being drawn from the relative safety of Zone Four, through the at-risk Zone Three, towards the danger of Zone Two into the critically dangerous Zone One.

The fact that this force is invisible and intangible does not mean it is imaginary or that there are no consequences attached to being drawn into Zone One. The corporate graveyards and hospitals are full of dead and dying companies that have graduated from Zone Four, to Three, through Two and finally into One.

Although this seems counter-intuitive, the contemporary tendency to overmanage has contributed to, rather than prevented, the exposure of modern companies to the risk of The Whirlpool Effect™. Unwittingly, the style and practice of so-called modern management has worked with rather than against the forces of the whirlpool.

In my experience, management has a strong focus on getting the job done, rather than on the people who contribute to the objectives, goals and purpose of the company. Sure, management likes to think that they have a vision or mission in place. They like to think that this is supported by a clear strategy with underlying tactical plans, and that the organisational structure is elegantly designed to achieve the desired outcomes.

They fantasise constantly about how the organisational structure can be refined, remodelled or even re-engineered whenever the desired outcomes seem unlikely to be achieved — or even more perplexingly, when they are likely to be achieved. I am amazed at the obsession modern management has with organisational structure, failing to realise that frequently it is the single most important impediment to achievement of long-term goals and ultimately the purpose of the company.

Most modern management is really focused on the short term and pays lip-service to sustainable longer-term achievements.

A busy manager with a full in-tray, fourteen new messages on their cellphone, an overcommitted diary stretching weeks into the future and a line manager who resigned the day before yesterday, might justifiably feel less than focused on the long term. However, it is their natural inclination to give their attention to those non-value or low-value-added, short-term issues that appear urgent only on the day, that is a major contributor to the progression of their company towards the centre of the whirlpool. This focus on short-term, non-value-added activities is what so easily disorientates them and causes them to lose their key landmarks. Before they know it, they are caught in the downstream current.

This is not to say that there are not value-added components which do have a short-term orientation. My concern is that short-term issues, which by their nature are more often than not non-value-added to low-value-added, tend to submerge short-term objectives which are the most value-added short-term element. What is important is to create a balance between value-added short-term objectives and the longer-term goals and purpose of the company.

It is not only the way modern management operates that endangers their companies, it is also the way they think. Their innate belief in the power of logic overwhelms their relationships with their employees. If something makes sense to the modern manager, it must make sense to the employee. The modern manager talks about innovation and expects employees to be innovative, but more often than not creates an environment where authority is not matched with responsibility. It is not possible to be innovative in this type of environment which is fundamentally a bureaucracy.

THE GRIM DETERMINATION OF BUREAUCRACY

ONE DAY I WAS RUNNING LATE AS I TRAVELLED FROM MY office to an appointment across the city. Intent on minimising my lateness and deep in concentration, I was taken aback, as I drove around a bend, by an orange light flashing from the back of a white station wagon, whose tailgate was open.

I had read a few months earlier about the introduction of speed cameras and thought to myself that I had been captured by one of these. I forgot about the incident until a week later, when a serious brown envelope, marked 'Police, Speed Camera Division', turned up in my mailbox.

Once inside I opened the envelope to find a large, high-quality colour picture of my car and me. I was momentarily impressed — until I saw the fine. I thought about what I should do for some days and then decided that I needed closure on this matter.

I took out my chequebook and wrote a cheque for the required amount. Then I fetched my camera and took a picture of the cheque. The next day I took the film to a photographic laboratory and asked them to develop it to the same size, colour and quality of the speed camera picture which with some embarrassment I showed to them.

They did a fine job. I went out and bought a serious brown envelope and placed the picture of the cheque inside it and sent it to 'Police, Speed Camera Division'.

I was rather impressed with myself and told anyone who was prepared to listen what I had done. As you would expect, within a very short period of time there were less and less people who wished to hear my story. The matter of my speed camera ticket faded rapidly from my memory and happily for family, friends and acquaintances, from my conversation.

About two weeks later I was taken aback to find a serious brown envelope, marked 'Police, Speed Camera Division' on the top right-hand corner, in my mailbox. With unbearable curiosity I rushed inside to examine the contents of the envelope. I found a large, high-quality colour photograph . . . it was . . . a photograph of . . .

. . . A PAIR OF HANDCUFFS!

This apocryphal tale shows that no matter how creative and innovative you try to be, the grim determination of bureaucracy will get you.

The modern manager generally thinks that bureaucracy is somewhere else, usually in government or some other central administration. Sometimes they think bureaucracy is alive and well in their head office, or within the organisations of their competitors and possibly even their suppliers. They seldom, if ever, think it is within their own organisation, lovingly and often unknowingly nurtured by themselves.

Bureaucracy is everywhere. It is in central and local government. It is in the not-for-profit sector. But it is as alive and well in the private sector, in companies large, medium and small.

Not all, but most employees know that it is there. Customers definitely know it is there.

The attributes of bureaucracy — which are primarily oppressiveness and inflexibility — are in my view a result of organisations and companies being overmanaged and underled. Bureaucracy is the single greatest impediment to innovation and empowerment. Without innovation and empowerment it is unlikely that an organisation or company can ever achieve its true potential.

Bureaucracy is a disease of modern management; a dangerous disease that debilitates organisations or companies and can ultimately be the major contributing factor to their untimely death.

What worries me about bureaucracy is that it is highly transmissible. It is transferred from lecturers to students, from boards to chief executives, senior managers to line managers, line managers to employees. Managers, particularly at a senior level when they shift from one organisation or company to another, can carry the disease of bureaucracy with them, rapidly infecting their new organisation.

Sadly, small- to medium-sized exciting emerging companies are at great risk of being infected with this disease when they merge with or are taken over by larger, more traditional companies.

Power, the desire for ascendancy and control, is at the core of modern management's lack of insight and remoteness.

The underlying problem with modern management is that it relies on skills and ideas which have outlived their relevance. Customers know this, employees know this . . . but strangely, much of management does not.

It is because modern management has become disconnected from employees, who as a consequence have become disconnected to varying degrees from the customers. You would think that the modern manager with their breadth of education and experience would have the insight to identify this disconnection. But the majority do not. They are remote and disconnected not because they lack interest, commitment or intelligence. The fundamental reason is something that most people in management do not wish to confront. Everyone knows about it; employees definitely know about it, and customers bear the consequences of it. I am talking about the 'P' word.

Power, the desire for ascendancy and control, is at the core of modern management's lack of insight and remoteness. It is the underlying cause of the disconnection that I have described.

The desire for power is driven by varying degrees of self-interest, self-conceit and systemic selfishness. I have heard many people say that you cannot be a top manager without an ego. If by that people mean having a sense of individuality, then I can agree. However, I think the reality is that they are talking not about ego but about egotism.

If power and egotism, however covert, are key drivers of modern management's mindset, decision-making, organisational perspective and view on managing personnel and resources, then it is not unsurprising that our organisations and companies are overmanaged and underled.

There has been, and continues to be, debate and disagreement about the difference between managers and leaders. This debate has escalated over the last two decades as the issue has become more relevant with the declining performance of a number of organisations and companies across a wide range of industry sectors. There has been a greater emphasis on management education and training over the last two decades than at any other time. Has this education and training translated into improved performance for organisations and companies?

I have strong doubts that it has. In fact I have a real concern that the opposite may have been achieved. The emphasis on management rather than on leadership has, in retrospect, been an error of significant proportion. It is leadership that has the capacity to forge sustainable, flourishing organisations and companies — not management.

> **The distinction between leadership and management is an important one and should be made with great clarity.**

The distinction between management and leadership can be presented as varying shades of grey and often is. This too is a mistake. The distinction between leadership and management is an important one and should be made with great clarity.

❧ THE MANAGEMENT OLYMPICS

I WAS TRAVELLING IN A BUS WITH A NUMBER OF colleagues. As we were travelling a long distance, we were passing the time by debating amongst ourselves a number of business-related topics.

At one point the discussion was about how you would determine who the best manager was. We were not really reaching any relevant conclusions, when an elderly man sitting in the row behind tapped my colleague sitting alongside me, on the left shoulder.

The elderly man excused himself for interrupting. He went on to say that he could not help but overhear our conversation. He asked if he could contribute his view. My colleague seemed a little frustrated at having our discussion interrupted, but as a courtesy asked the man to proceed.

Although this happened many years ago, I have never forgotten what he said.

He said: 'I could not help listening to you bright young men and women talking amongst yourselves. You obviously have all enjoyed an excellent education and hold interesting opinions about business.

'Even though I am now an old man I am still interested in what makes the world go around. I know nothing about business at all. I have never been in business. I have never been a manager, I have never even owned a single share on the stockmarket.

'My whole life has been spent in sports. I represented my country in the Olympic Games many years ago, possibly before any of you were born. I do not mean to sound boastful, but I won the gold medal in my event. I was quite simply the best in the world at that time.

'When I retired from my chosen active sport I became a coach and have been associated with both winners and losers ever since.

'Early in my career as a coach my charges were much less successful than later on when they became winners on a consistent basis. In the early part of my career when a number of my charges were less successful than they should have been I became very despondent. After having been the best at what I did, I was now becoming a failure. I could not understand why, as I was careful to ensure that my charges prepared themselves in the exact same way that I had.

'I approached the man who had been my coach and sought his advice.

'He asked me whether I thought I had any leadership capability. I said that I did not understand how this related to my problem.

'He replied that it had everything to do with my problem. I had paid attention only to the management side of my role as the coach. I had totally neglected to provide my charges with the leadership they needed.

'My charges were fit and had exceptional technique. We had also planned to the last tactical detail. But as my old coach had pointed out, I had prepared only the body and the mind and had paid no attention to the heart and the soul.

'To win, you need the heart and the soul as well as the body and the mind.

'I changed my approach, placing the emphasis on the heart and soul, and my losers became winners.

'Like I said, I am an old man and I know nothing about business, but I think that to answer your question the best manager is actually the best leader. So if you want to have your contest for the best manager, you should not look at the managers, you should look at the people who work for them. The best manager will be the one who has the strongest, most focused and best organised following.

'Another thing that always fascinated me when I was a sportsman and a coach, was how good some people were at their sport. Looking outside my own sport, I always marvelled at the strength of the weightlifters, the speed of the sprinters and the agility of the gymnasts.

'I myself was an excellent sportsman, a proven world champion. However, there was no way that I could lift half the weight of the champion weightlifter. I would have been less than half way down the 100 yards track when the champions would have been finished, and I could not even do a coordinated forward roll.

'There are people who by virtue of their heredity, experience, natural ability and hard work will be champions. In my field of sport only the best made the Olympics. They needed to first be champions in their age group, then of their city, then of their state or country before they could come to the Olympics.

'It strikes me that there is no organised contest for the best manager, and although I know nothing about management and business I would bet that there are similarities with sport.

'There will be managers in business who will have the right background and experience matched with natural ability and hard work. They will be the champions.

'Just like the champion weightlifters, sprinters and gymnasts, there will be managers who have incredible judgment, intellect and leadership capability. They are quite simply better than other managers and that is how life is. They are the leaders and they are the people who will win your contest.'

The importance of leadership in the management of organisations and companies must be made explicit. If there is a lesson to be learned from this tale, it is to confront the fact that while any number of people can participate, only a few can be champions. *My view on success is not defined by meeting targets, rather by fulfilling potential.* There can be a significant difference between the two.

❧ A LARGE LEAP FOR LEADERSHIP

In the 1968 Mexico Olympic Games, an athlete called Bob Beamon won the gold medal for the men's long jump. Not only did he win the event, he broke the world record by an amazing 21 inches (55cm). This was, and continues to be, one of the most astonishing athletic feats of all time.

It is usual for a new record to be set in very small increments. For the long jump this may be less than half an inch (less than one centimetre). Beamon jumped 29 feet 2 1/2 inches (8.90 metres) when nobody had approached even 28 feet (8.53 metres) before. His competitors included the previous joint record-holders as well as the previous Olympic champion. This was a competition of the best of the best.

I followed the 1968 Olympics as a teenager and this feat has had an ongoing impact on my life. I still have a memory of Bob Beamon hanging in the air, determined in his battle against gravity. His jump was not just a jump it was a leap of logic which had consequences way beyond the sport of long jumping and the Olympic movement. It is one of the more significant events to illustrate that if we focus on the opportunity of potential rather than the limitation of targets, who knows how far we can go.

Leadership is different from management because it does focus on the achievement of potential for individuals, organisations or companies, industry sectors, communities, and indeed whole countries. For an organisation or company to have the remotest opportunity of reaching its potential it needs to operate outside the forces of the whirlpool, in Zone Five.

It is leadership, not management, that will secure a place for an organisation or company in the placid waters outside the whirlpool's grasp.

TWO | PRACTICAL APPLICATION OF THE WHIRLPOOL EFFECT™

Yes, we see it, but it is so uncomfortable that we can't admit to it.

— Gary Hamel

The Whirlpool Effect™ is not merely a theoretical concept — it has a practical application that can assist managers to make their organisations more effective.

The first thing The Whirlpool Effect™ does is to cast aside the bad 'P' word . . . Power. This has no place in the development of an organisation or company that is attempting to truly meet its potential.

The Whirlpool Effect™ does, however, embrace the good 'P' words:

- Purpose
- Planning
- Process
- People

Purpose, Planning, Process and People form the cornerstones of The Whirlpool Effect™ and are the building blocks for the leadership of any organisation or company.

To optimise results from the application of The Whirlpool Effect™, these four elements need to be in balance and equilibrium. This is critical and any positive outcomes are dependent on achieving it. In an environment where Purpose, Planning and Process are at an optimum, the entire organisation or company could, for example, still be at risk because of less than ideal circumstances in relation to the fourth element, People.

Each of the four cornerstone elements is further divided into six sub-elements. These sub-elements summarise my views on the essential attributes of leadership. They are represented in The Whirlpool Effect™ model as coordinates arranged at every fifteen degrees of each cornerstone, and are called *lines of leadership*.

As a consequence, there are six lines of leadership for each cornerstone and twenty-four for the entire Whirlpool Effect™. The diagram on page 33 represents the balance and equilibrium of the four cornerstones, the lines of leadership and their numerical allocation.

There are no weightings at all for any of the lines of leadership. While some lines of leadership may seem to claim more importance than others, and should as a consequence attract a greater weighting, it is important that they do not. A critical underlying principle of The Whirlpool Effect™ and its application is the balance and equilibrium that it demands of managers.

Consistency is essential to allow coherent comparisons and replication of results between, say, a portfolio of companies, departments in an organisation or company, or branches of the same company or organisation.

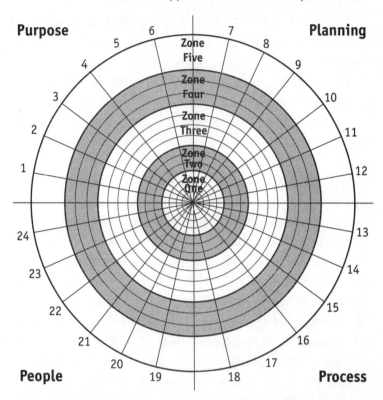

KEY:	
Zone One:	*Tornado*
Zone Two:	*Powerful Gale*
Zone Three:	*Strong Winds with Unpredictably Powerful Gusts*
Zone Four:	*Mild to Moderate Winds*
Zone Five:	*Placid*

The numbers 1–24 refer to the lines of leadership. See The Whirlpool Effect™ survey in Part 7 for descriptions of each of the lines of leadership.

The Whirlpool Effect™ model has the ability to diagnose two important factors critical to the health of any organisation or company.

Firstly, it has the ability to diagnose the level of connection or disconnection between management and employees. The connection between management and employees in a balanced way across each of the four cornerstones is essential in providing exceptional service and satisfaction to customers.

It is not possible on any sustainable or consistent basis to provide exceptional service if disconnections are present. The greater the degree of disconnection, the higher the level of dysfunctionality likely within the organisation or company. The greater the degree of dysfunctionality, the greater the negative impact on the customer.

Secondly, The Whirlpool Effect™ model is able to identify the zone in which the organisation or company finds itself. From this it is possible to determine the level of safety or danger the company or organisation faces.

From a practical perspective, The Whirlpool Effect™ depends on a visual analogue survey of management and employees. Each group is asked to identify their view on the organisation's or company's performance in relation to each of the twenty-four lines of leadership. Every person completing the survey would need to complete only twenty-four questions, of which the following is an example:

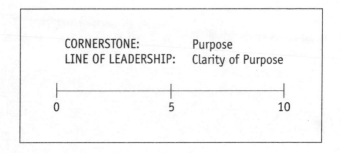

If the person completing this question felt that there was no clarity of purpose at all, they would select zero. If on the other hand they felt that there was absolute clarity of purpose, they would select ten. However, if they felt it was somewhere part way between zero and ten, they would select the point that they felt best represented their perception, which is in fact the reality. The complete survey is in Part 7 on page 189.

Following the completion of the surveys, an analysis is undertaken separating management and employees into two separate groups. The median score for each line of leadership for the two separate groups is then plotted on The Whirlpool Effect™ model, an example of which follows on page 36.

This example demonstrates a close alignment and as a consequence a strong connection between management and employees in relation to the Planning cornerstone. Both sets of results are comfortably in Zone Four.

There is a moderate disconnection between management and employees in the Process cornerstone. The employees have identified the mid part of Zone Three, while management has identified a position close to the safest part of Zone Four.

There are major disconnections between management and employees in both the Purpose and People cornerstones. Of major concern is that the employee survey results for Purpose are in Zone One while that of management are in Zone Four, bordering on Zone Five. The disconnection for the People cornerstone, while still significant, is not of the same magnitude with the employees' results identifying Zone Two and management identifying Zone Four, bordering on Zone Three.

This organisation faces significant danger unless the gap between its employees' views on Purpose and People and that of management can be altered.

In my experience this mapped model is reasonably typical of many organisations. What is really intriguing is that most

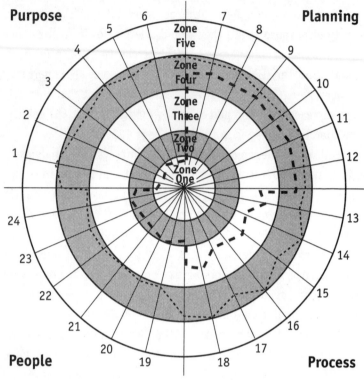

KEY LINES:

– – – · Employees

·········· Management

KEY:	
Zone One:	*Tornado*
Zone Two:	*Powerful Gale*
Zone Three:	*Strong Winds with Unpredictably Powerful Gusts*
Zone Four:	*Mild to Moderate Winds*
Zone Five:	*Placid*

organisations like this will be expending valuable time, energy and financial resources in Planning and Process re-engineering, when in reality these are not the areas of the imminent risks or dangers that the organisation or company faces.

The most compelling advantage of The Whirlpool Effect™ model is that it confronts management myopia and denial by clearly identifying disconnections between management and employees.

This example illustrates a company that lacks leadership and the emphasis needs to be placed on Purpose and People as a priority. The diagnostic ability of The Whirlpool Effect™ model allows an organisation or company to prioritise already scarce resources into the areas where they will achieve the maximum benefit.

The most compelling advantage of The Whirlpool Effect™ model is that it confronts management myopia and denial by clearly identifying disconnections between management and employees. These disconnections are fundamental drivers of below-average performance and the inability to meet potential. Unfortunately, the denial is often most powerful at the top of the organisation or company. Perhaps this is why Gary Hamel, a professor at the London Business School, has talked in the past about the need for gene replacement therapy for top management!

Gene replacement therapy for managers is a nice concept, but unlikely to happen. The Whirlpool Effect™ model is a realistic and practical way of encouraging managers to recognise and accept these important disconnections, no matter how uncomfortable it is for them personally.

PART 2
PURPOSE

I HAVE A DREAM...

THREE | **SEE IT AS IT IS LIKELY TO BE, NOT AS YOU WOULD LIKE IT TO BE**

Leaders must invoke an alchemy of great vision. Those who do not are ultimately judged failures.

— Henry Kissinger

In management, as in all walks of life, language is important. The management literature is bedevilled by the inappropriate use of language and managers do not reflect sufficiently on their choice of important words. The inappropriate use of language by managers, in my experience, serves only to fuel cynicism amongst employees.

It all started with the development of an organisation or company's 'mission'. Mission statements flourished in annual reports and in corporate literature and you could hardly visit an organisation or company without seeing a framed mission statement hanging behind the reception counter. A mission is defined as a task or a goal and the journey undertaken as part of this. I think the choice of the word 'mission' as the potentially driving and inspiring force, compelling an organisation or company forward, was a disastrous choice.

> I think the choice of the word 'mission' as the potentially driving and inspiring force, compelling an organisation or company forward, was a disastrous choice.

'Mission' signifies, to me, and to most employees I have spoken to, something at a lower level than the word that seems to have supplanted mission . . . 'vision'.

'Vision' is defined as a mental picture, an imaginative insight, statesman-like foresight or something seen in a dream. I have to confess to have been somewhat of a devotee of vision. Vision seemed so much more superior to mission, something much more than task- or goal-directed. I regarded the development of a powerful and inspiring vision as one of the most important attributes of a leader.

I used to describe a vision as 'a dream with a plan'. The vision was a reality that the leader could sense and could then inspire concurrent feelings of enthusiasm, hope and commitment amongst the employees in the organisation or company.

I came to believe that the ability to develop a vision that clarified a picture of the future and inspired individuals to contribute to realising that future was perhaps the major factor distinguishing a leader from a manager.

🐚 'I HAVE A DREAM'

WHEN DR MARTIN LUTHER KING JR STOOD BEFORE HIS people, he did not say, 'I have a strategic plan.' He said, 'I have a dream.'

This was something that I often used when I was talking to line managers or employees, to emphasise the difference between capturing people's hearts and souls as opposed to just their minds.

It certainly captured their attention and I was impressed with myself. I thought that I had found an excellent mechanism for differentiating between the leadership attribute of possessing and developing a vision, and the management attribute of planning.

My perception of a vision as a dream with a plan could link the powerful, emotive imagery of a great leader like Martin Luther King with the duller, more mundane technical process of planning. Like many managers, I went about my business, relishing my ability to develop, communicate and win commitment to the vision.

I was working as chief executive of South Auckland Health at the time. It was a time of significant public sector reform in health. Despite the fact that my organisation was making very good progress, the reform process itself was experiencing some reasonably major difficulties. I took time to carefully think through where things might have gone wrong.

The reform process did commence with a vision, but as the political reality dawned, the builders built to a set of plans quite different to those developed by the original architect of the vision. This resulted in the perception amongst the majority of people in the sector that health reform was, in their experience, not a vision but an hallucination.

I began to wonder about the concept of vision, developing doubts about something in which I had held such strong beliefs. I set out to gain an understanding of how employees in different organisations or companies perceived their visions.

> I was alarmed and depressed by what I found. The majority of employees I spoke to felt their companies' visions, too, were hallucinations.
>
> At the core of developing a vision is the need to inspire employees to commit themselves to achieve an organisation's or company's potential. If employees view senior management's vision as a hallucination, it may well have the exact opposite effect.
>
> I was confused . . . maybe we need something stronger and more tangible than a dream.

My discussions with a range of employees from many different companies across a number of industry sectors was very revealing. It not only reinforced to me the disconnection between management and employees, it also opened my eyes to the lack of management credibility.

These discussions left me with a desire to replace the word 'vision'. My background work on vision had usually been with managers. This was the first time that I had immersed myself totally with employees in a debate on vision, throwing aside all the curses of assumption that I previously had held.

What a fascinating experience it was. The feedback I had is that employees do want something to which they can truly commit, something that draws them and their organisation towards it, like a magnet. Whatever it is, they said it needs to be clear, relevant, understood, inspiring ... but more than anything else it needs to be *shared*.

❧ WHEN THE APPLE HITS YOU ON THE HEAD

I CAN NOW SEE HOW EASY IT WAS FOR ISAAC NEWTON TO determine that gravity existed, when the apple fell off the tree and hit him on the head. I experienced a similar feeling when talking with these various employees. Their big problem with 'mission' and 'vision' was that they were generally never involved.

The more I thought of it, the more I realised that every time a senior management group needs to develop a vision or a strategic plan, they generally go to a place called a 'retreat'. This 'retreat' is invariably a superior or luxury hotel or resort, generally a long distance from the organisation or company. It is almost as if senior management needs to escape 'the workers' so that they can get on with these matters of such major import. It is as if 'the workers' affected the oxygen in the air, diminishing senior management's ability to think and plan.

If you have to go to one of those things called a 'retreat', and I personally do not think you do, at least call it an 'advance'.

It is really so simple. Employees in a company do not respond positively to someone coming down from the mountain with two tablets of stone, with the prescription for the organisation's or company's future engraved upon them.

The apple on the head that I experienced is that the problem modern management has stems from the fact that the mission or vision is seen by the average employee as being associated with the board of directors, chief executive, or the senior management team. It does not appear to them to be something that belongs to the organisation or company, independent of the senior executive, something that they can truly share.

I have read in relation to the concept of employee buy-in and commitment, that once employees have committed to the leader's vision, they begin to participate in shaping it and at this point it becomes shared. A true leader does not create a vision and gift it to an organisation, which then has an opportunity to participate and share. This is why I believe we should no longer use the word 'vision'. We need a word that implies a real sense of ownership by the organisation or company. The word I prefer to use is *purpose*.

Purpose is defined as an object to be attained, intention to act or a thing intended. One of the reasons I like the word is that it does not sound as frivolous as 'mission' or 'vision'. Frankly, it is not management-speak and is thus much more appealing and acceptable to employees, who are, after all, the most important group in any organisation or company.

Purpose has a connotation of strength, action and direction and as a consequence I have selected it as one of the four cornerstones of The Whirlpool Effect™. In my mind, the purpose clarifies the destination point for that organisation or company. It is important that it creates a clear, credible, relevant and understandable future. This is really a longer-range target that inspires individuals to act collectively to reach the destination.

In a very real sense the purpose defines the journey from where the organisation or company is now, to its destination.

Modern management tends to place such a strong emphasis on where it is going, characterised often by a vague vision or mission statement, that it neglects to understand its current position. When I was out and about amongst employees in a wide range of companies across various industries, I would ask individuals to write in longhand their interpretation of where the organisation or company was currently situated. Interestingly, it was unusual for more than a few people to have a perfectly aligned view. But most management remains blissfully unaware of these critical disconnections.

I would also ask individuals to write in longhand their interpretation of where the organisation or company was heading. Again, it was unusual for more than a few people to have a perfectly aligned view.

I do not think it is possible to define a credible and relevant destination point or a purpose if there is no sense of clarity as to the starting point.

The starting point for the development or refinement of any organisation's or company's purpose, is not the conference room at a luxury hotel or resort. It is in the heart of the organisation, working with the employees to ensure first that there is a clear and shared understanding of where the organisation or company is currently placed. This needs to be done in detail and needs to create a strong mental image, as it is easier to share an understanding of something pictorial.

Only when there is agreement on the current position can one focus on the development of the future position, the purpose and then the plan for the journey.

❧ IT IS THE JOURNEY, NOT THE DESTINATION

I DO NOT PLAY THE GAME OF GOLF ALTHOUGH I OFTEN WISH I did — not only for the challenge and enjoyment, but because golf can provide many lessons in management.

In the game of golf, the purpose is clear. For each hole, you start from the tee and end by sinking a putt and the fewer strokes you take the better. It is absolutely clear to anyone who plays the game of golf at a particular course, on a particular hole, where the starting point is and what the destination is.

Different players with differing skills and abilities will have different journeys from the tee shot to the hole. The person who hits the best first shot will not necessarily be the person who achieves the lowest number of strokes in reaching the hole.

In golf, as in management, once the starting point and the destination are clear to all involved, it is the journey that becomes much more important than the destination.

I do not know for sure, but I suspect the reason that modern management is so strongly focused on the destination has nothing to do with the organisation or company. I think it has almost everything to do with the managers themselves and their desire for rapid personal achievements.

You cannot be motivated by self-interest and expect to be a leader.

The purpose of genuinely inspiring employees has to be more that just something about numbers. Even accountants want to commit to something compelling, something worth doing. The trouble with too many of modern management's missions, visions, call them what you like, is that they do not even hint at a future any different from the present. This is because they are too focused on the numbers — once again managers are trying to capture the mind, rather than the heart.

An effective purpose will emotionally connect with the employee, with their heart and with their soul, and then they will put their mind to making it happen. I believe strongly from my experience that inspiration touches people's hearts and souls which then energises their minds, channelling their power into the muscles of the organisation.

> **The trouble with too many of modern management's missions, visions, call them what you like, is that they do not even hint at a future any different from the present.**

A purpose is not about logic, it is about emotion, passion, enthusiasm and optimism . . . it is about what *can* be done, not about what *must* be done.

The purpose is not fundamentally about profit or any financial target. Profit is important but is a consequence of the purpose, not the purpose itself.

❧ MONEY AND SNOW

A COLLEAGUE OF MINE WAS INVOLVED IN A NEGOTIATION IN Canada with a First Nation tribe on a health-related issue. She was leading a team that had prepared a number of financial instruments to assist in the development of First Nation health projects.

She was negotiating with the tribal chief through an interpreter. The negotiations did not appear to be making progress. One of her team members asked if he could request a recess.

During the recess the team member, who had some

understanding of the First Nation language, said that every time she mentioned one of the different financial instruments, the interpreter translated it into the First Nation word for money. My colleague was not surprised the negotiations were not making progress, as the chief was not deriving the benefit of all the background work they had done to develop a wide choice of financial modalities to structure the health projects.

Prior to the negotiations recommencing, my colleague called the interpreter aside and expressed her concern about the way he was translating all of these quite different financial instruments, each presenting quite different opportunities, simply as 'money'. She wanted to know how the chief would ever get an understanding of the opportunities they were presenting and how he could possibly make an informed decision.

The interpreter, keen to give the impression that he was doing a good job, explained carefully that to the First Nation people money was not that important and consequently they only had one word for it. Whether it was debt, equity, subordinated debt, a debt-equity swap or a partial subsidy was irrelevant in their language — it was all just money.

The interpreter went on to explain that other things were more important to the First Nation people and they had, for example, many words to describe snow.

This story has relevance to any management situation involving purpose. Like the First Nation people, most employees understand the place of money and profit, but there are more important things to them. If the purpose is only about financial achievement, you will find you will have as much luck sustaining an understandable conversation with employees as my colleague had with the First Nation chief.

Let us be absolutely clear — profit is important to all organisations. It is not only important to companies in the private sector; it is equally important to not-for-profit and public sector organisations. Privately owned organisations may distribute their surpluses in a different way from not-for-profit, welfare or public sector organisations, but their need for surpluses is the same. Not-for-profit, in my book, does not mean 'for loss' as many of our public sector organisations have chosen to operate, causing governments to alter their expenditure priorities. A profit or surplus is required to attract and retain the best employees and to invest in technology and capital development.

❧ BODIES AND BALANCE SHEETS

I HAVE ADAPTED HERE THE FASCINATING DESCRIPTION OF the role of profit that I once read in a book titled *Strategy Pure and Simple*, by Michel Robert.

The human body needs food to fuel its system — if you do not eat, you will ultimately starve to death. This is a fact: you need to eat to live. But however important food may be to the body, almost no one I know lives solely for the purpose of eating.

An organisation or company needs profit to fuel its system. Without sustainable surpluses the company will wither and ultimately die. This is a fact: organisations or companies need cash to live. However, just like the human body, no organisation should exist solely for the purpose of making a profit.

> Henry Ford, early in the twentieth century, said 'Wealth, like happiness, is never attained when sought after directly. It comes as a byproduct of providing a useful service.'

The purpose should not focus purely on the numbers. To be compelling it does not have to be magical or mystical; it does, however, need to be inspiring.

Having defined where the organisation or company is and where it is going, the purpose supplies the ground rules for leading the journey. It is important, though, not only to work forward from the present, but also to work backward from the future . . . a talent and ability that only leaders have.

 **FOUR** | **SPEAK LESS, SAY MORE**

You cannot command commitment, you can
only inspire it.

— Thomas Stewart

Purpose, while formed around the organisation or company and led by the man or woman at the top, will not achieve its potential if it is not made personal to the individual employee in some meaningful way.

🌀 WE CAN GET YOUR RADIO STATION HERE

In every organisation and company, in every department and at every level in the organisation, not only across communities, but across countries and the world, all employees are tuned into the same radio station.

You have heard it, it is called Station WIIFM . . . What's In It For Me?

Each individual employee is the most important thing to themselves. This does not mean that they are selfish, or self-absorbed. What it does mean is they want to be in the frame, to be involved, to be part of the whole.

An effective purpose must convey to each and every employee the clear and compelling message that their work (no matter which level they are at) is important, makes a valuable contribution and is part of the collective outcome.

It is important, though, that individual employees can test their own efforts and achievements against the purpose. This allows them to determine whether what they are doing as individuals, sweeping the floor or developing superconductors, is supportive of the overall purpose.

❧ WHO ARE WE WORKING FOR?

IMAGINE ONE DAY YOUR BOSS TAKES YOU AND YOUR co-workers on a surprise outing. You all clamber on the bus with the first stop being the city's tallest, gleaming tower building.

Your boss leads you into the cathedral-like entrance, taking you up in the marble-lined high speed lifts to the top floor. He shows you around the sumptuous boardroom and the chief executive's huge, beautifully designed office with a fantastic view overlooking the harbour.

He then leads you through the executive gymnasium and restaurant where chefs prepare customised meals, down to the carpark to view the chief executive's luxury European car.

You all clamber back onto the bus which travels through

the most affluent suburb and stops outside a beautiful Georgian mansion, which he points out belongs to the chief executive whose offices you have recently visited. The bus then travels to the local marina where your boss spends a less-than-riveting ten minutes, pointing out every minute detail of the chief executive's 20 metre yacht.

You all get onto the bus and travel back to work. After disembarking from the bus he assembles the group in the meeting room. Your boss stands before the group and says, 'The reason I have taken you out today and shown you the things that I have, is to indicate to you very clearly, that if you all absolutely commit yourself to our purpose, if you go beyond the extra mile, by working harder than you do currently, then one day all of what I have just shown you will be . . . **MINE**'!

No individual employee that I know wants to commit themselves and work hard only for the leader's own programme to succeed.

A purpose must be demanding and challenging — and not easily achievable — otherwise the potential of the organisation or company will not be tested. But this is not enough; there needs to be a real sense of contribution felt by each individual employee.

A purpose is a call to action, seeking a collective outcome from a disparate group of individuals.

I have already discussed the importance of purpose being *shared*, *relevant* and *clear*

> **No individual employee that I know wants to commit themselves and work hard only for the leader's own programme to succeed.**

which are the first three lines of leadership in The Whirlpool Effect™ model's cornerstone of purpose. I will now place more emphasis on the other three lines of leadership related to the Purpose cornerstone . . . that the purpose must be *inspiring*, *understood* and *credible*.

❧ BAD NEWS . . . YOU HAVE TO BE BETTER THAN NELSON MANDELA

FEW PEOPLE WOULD DISAGREE THAT NELSON MANDELA IS one of the greatest, if not the greatest, leaders of the current millennium. Mandela has achieved in South Africa what the majority of people, both inside and outside the country, thought was unachievable.

Mandela and several of his supporters made huge personal sacrifices — in the case of Mandela, 29 years in prison — to ensure that their shared purpose, of being free people, became so compelling. Their sacrifice, inspired by Mandela, became a cumulative force among black people in South Africa. The purpose became so powerful because Mandela had made it *clear* (the destination was one person/ one vote), *understandable* and *relevant*.

As time passed this purpose was shared as each individual was bound by a similar commitment and aspiration. I believe the reason this purpose was so overwhelming was not only because it was clear, understandable, relevant and shared, but particularly because Mandela himself had made it so inspiring and credible.

As Max Dupree has said, 'a leader's job is to absorb pain, not inflict it.' Mandela had certainly done this. He had made the whole purpose so believable by his sacrifice to the cause. The cause was always more important than him as its leader — a position he has continued to this day.

Gayle Hamilton has been quoted as saying, 'You can't follow someone who isn't credible, who doesn't truly believe in what they're doing — and how they're doing it.'

It is true that Mandela did have some things going for him. To create loyalty around the purpose of being free men and women is definitely easier than gaining a common commitment to a purpose of delivering courier packages on time, selling curtain rails, baking bread within tight specifications, assembling bicycles to precision tolerances or marketing pet flea collars to a budget.

As managers, however, we need to be better than Nelson Mandela . . . that is a benchmark that will truly test our potential.

The real question that faces modern management is how to inspire employees about something that is relatively ordinary. John F Kennedy also had it pretty good — landing man on the moon for the first time is something that most people could commit to. If it is something out of the ordinary, or new and different, it is easier to stir powerful human emotions, which is a great help in building a shared commitment. This is why the role of the leader in an organisation or company dealing with relatively ordinary, or well accepted, products and

The real question that faces modern management is how to inspire employees about something that is relatively ordinary.

services needs to have exceptional skills of persuasion and communication.

It is reasonably unlikely that many employees would be inspired by something they did not understand. I think it is possible, however, by sheer personality, enthusiasm and optimism, to inspire people about something they do not necessarily feel all that strongly about, or maybe initially do not even believe in. But if they do not understand it you are unlikely to be able to inspire them.

One of the main reasons why purposes that pass the test for clarity, relevance and credibility, and are shared and inspiring, still fail is because they are not understood.

Modern management often blames failure of purpose on what they like to call 'employee resistance to change'. In my experience, this is often an oversimplification and a shift of blame from management to employees. The main reason for the failure is the inability of management to adequately communicate the purpose.

Communication is not a one-way information flow, someone telling someone something or giving it to them in writing. Communication requires listening by both parties as well as the interaction which helps develop an understanding.

In my experience, of the three elements that comprise communication — talking, listening and understanding — poor or inadequate listening is the major cause of failure to communicate. Without listening it becomes very

> **In my experience, of the three elements that compromise communication — talking, listening and understanding — poor or inadequate listening is the major cause of failure to communicate.**

difficult to set up the interaction required.

Many authors on the subject of success in business have identified undercommunication as a problem related to the sharing of vision or purpose. I agree with this if by under-communication they mean under-listening. I cannot see how any manager can win any employee's commitment to something that employee does not clearly understand. Communication — making the purpose understandable — is the critical link in the move forward.

❧ IF THE TREE FALLS

YOU HAVE PROBABLY HEARD THE OLD QUESTION, 'IF A TREE falls in the forest, and there is no one in the forest to hear it, does it still make a sound?'

The answer is obviously yes.

Sound is a sensation caused by the vibration of the surrounding air. These vibrations occur, for example, when a tree falls in the forest, regardless of whether there is anyone there to hear it.

One of the most important skills a leader needs to have or develop is the skill of listening. A leader needs to hear sound when people are talking and needs also to be able to sense what is said when he or she is not present. Organisations and companies are like trees in the forest — there will be sounds when no one is present, but the leader needs to have a sixth sense to pick these up. True leaders have exceptional sensory ability.

It is essential to clarify the difference between hearing and listening, a fundamental and critical understanding modern management needs to possess.

❧ HEARING IS PHYSIOLOGY, LISTENING IS MANAGEMENT

DEBORAH HOPEN SAID: 'HEARING IS THE ABILITY TO process transmitted sound waves, it is a neurological process. On the other hand, listening involves making sense out of what is heard. Good listening takes time, effort and energy. Indeed, active listening can be more stressful than active speaking.'

Leaders listen with what I call the third ear, which means carefully understanding what is being said. This is important, because the consequence of not listening with a third ear is to lose the opportunity to make a heart-to-heart connection between the manager and employee. This connection is critical to win commitment to the purpose.

One of the techniques that I developed during my management career was a concept I called Listening Clinics.

Simply, Listening Clinics, when I was chief executive, involved putting a specific time aside each week at a specific venue, where any employee in the whole organisation could come and speak to me about any matter at all.

This was an absolutely safe environment (no one would get into trouble for what they said). They could come as often as they liked, and many did. They could address subjects related to them, their workplace or parts of the organisation that they were not involved with. They could tell me about me, they could criticise me — and many did.

The venue was the boardroom. It is a place most regular employees never get invited to, let alone have the opportunity to be put in a position of superiority over the chief executive. My role at the Listening Clinic was to listen and only to speak to them if what they said required an answer or if they wanted me to speak.

They could elect to talk only, and have me listen and not respond, despite anything they said. Many took this opportunity. Try sitting down with somebody and let them say things to you, without an opportunity to respond. I admit that I struggled with this. People could come to the Listening Clinic merely to listen to what others were saying. I only went into recess with an individual employee if that employee signalled that they wanted to raise a confidential issue. This happened from time to time but we all know that in most organisations everyone knows everything that is going on.

When I was at school studying physics, I was taught that light travelled faster than sound. In every organisation that I have been exposed to, I have found that gossip breaks this physical principle . . . when it comes to gossip (I hate to tell this to physicists) sound travels much, much faster than light.

My experience with Listening Clinics is that at a time of change or new developments, the number of people attending rises significantly. At other times there may be only a few attendees and for some weeks on end, no people at all. Listening Clinics assisted me by having another line of communication with staff, allowed me to identify and address problems, acted as a crude barometer of staff satisfaction, but most of all, over years and years of using them, helped me to develop the ability not only to hear but more importantly to listen.

As you will find throughout this book, the four cornerstones and the 24 lines of leadership [see pp 33 and 36] of The Whirlpool

Effect™ are constantly interrelated. Listening not only helps with communication and consequently understanding, but also helps more than most managers realise with credibility.

❧ WHERE DO I KEEP MY HANDBAG?

DURING ONE OF MY EARLY LISTENING CLINICS WHEN I WAS chief executive of South Auckland Health, one of the cleaners raised the issue that she had nowhere to keep her handbag safely, while she got on with her job of cleaning.

This was a problem for her, because her handbag contained her purse and other valuables like her chequebook. Obviously she could not leave these and other necessary items at home, as she needed them during the day.

It was not a big request, to be able to bring your handbag to work.

She told me that for years the cleaners had been trying to get lockers for their handbags, but no one cared to listen to their problem. She told me what a hassle it was trying to clean while watching your bag. She said she did not expect anything to be done about it, but as I was the newly appointed chief executive and was having these Listening Clinics, she would at least tell me.

I arranged for lockers to be set in place for the cleaners. They came back to the Listening Clinic to tell me how good these lockers were because in addition to being able to store their bags safely, when they went on breaks they could store the expensive cleaning fluids in the lockers, so that no one would steal them.

There were a number of victories here:

- the cleaners had somewhere to store their personal valuables and belongings, which gave them a sense

> of security, but more importantly, a sense of dignity.
> - the hospital stopped having expensive cleaning fluids stolen and this saved money which could be more usefully channelled into caring for patients.
> - as chief executive, I had a credibility infusion. People talk — sound travels faster than light and myths and legends grow. I was seen as an action man, someone who cared about people whom management had previously disregarded.
> - the organisation had a workforce that became more committed, because it was seen as an organisation that cared.

Effective communication does require more than highly developed listening skills, particularly if it is to inspire individual employees. I do not know about you, but I do not feel particularly inspired, confident or even slightly moved if my leader stands in front of me and my fellow employees and proceeds to give a speech on an important matter to us — like our company being merged with another company — and she has to read from a written speech. To me, it seems like a message coming not from her heart and soul, possibly not even from her mind, but from some public relations speechwriter's pen.

To inspire people, you need to look them in the eye and speak to them from the heart. Modern management has lost it — you do not need Powerpoint presentations to communicate with and inspire your employees. The only prop you need is integrity, because all your

Studies have shown that the leadership attribute that employees admire most is honesty.

employees want to hear is the truth. Drop the cosmetics. Studies have consistently shown that the leadership attribute that employees admire most is honesty.

Honesty beats a number of other admirable attributes — such as competence, intelligence, courage, dependability, caring and loyalty — hands down.

Communication, to be effective, needs to be from the heart and it needs to be honest.

❀ IS VERBOSITY A COMPLIMENT?

I WAS ONCE INVOLVED IN SOME INDUSTRIAL NEGOTIATIONS with nurses. You might ask, was I chief executive at the time, and if so why would I get involved with the negotiations directly? This could affect the organisation's negotiating position — if a chief executive is in the negotiating room, you may find yourself in a position where you have to make a decision there and then.

Hey, I *was* chief executive, and the reason I was in the negotiating room was so that we *could* make decisions there and then.

It was the early phase of the negotiations; it was a little boring and I found myself a bit distracted. I was sitting next to a nurse and noticed a document she had in front of her which was actually almost in front of me. So I read it, I could not help it.

The document was about their high-level negotiation strategy. It was a common-sense approach, which I felt was going to help create an outcome that was win–win. What did take me aback, though, was that I read a little bit about myself on the page. Some quite nice things were said until I came to the part which suggested I used too much jargon which they often did not understand — and also that I was a bit verbose.

I reflected on this and decided they were definitely right about the jargon and since then I have tried to eliminate jargon from my vocabulary. I am now as jargon-free as I can possibly be and have almost eradicated management-speak and technobabble. They were right. Jargon creates mistrust and cynicism and distracts from the message.

The verbosity comment hurt, particularly when I found out what it meant when I checked it in the dictionary after negotiations closed that day. Verbosity means using more words than are actually needed. They were right about this too. Like most managers, I should have spoken less and said more.

Impress your daily crossword puzzle with your great, varied and idiosyncratic vocabulary. When you communicate with employees keep it really simple . . . this helps to make it understandable. Effective communication is simple communication, it is jargon-free, it is meaningful and it is understandable. To ensure a purpose is not under-communicated it needs 'reach and frequency' . . . it needs to reach across the total organisation, both horizontally and vertically.

Effective communication is simple communication, it is jargon-free, it is meaningful and it is understandable.

The message will also need repetition — constant repetition, hundreds, perhaps thousands of times in meetings large and small, formal presentations, kerbside conversations, newsletters, one-on-ones and on the e-mail.

The communication of a purpose must never be dry and logical, it must be rich with imagery. Developing an interesting theme by storytelling is a powerful communication force, as the core message becomes linked to key understandable and memorable images.

Choose your words and stories carefully, maintain consistency, but most of all, always be honest.

Even the most imaginative, powerful communication will be stopped dead in its tracks by what most employees I know consider the most important element of communication . . . non-verbal communication, or how you act and behave.

Even the most imaginative, powerful communication will be stopped dead in its tracks by what most employees I know consider the most important element of communication . . . non-verbal communication, or how you act and behave. If top management lives the purpose and the values of the organisation, those troublesome questions about credibility do not arise, grow, and become a major problem. The old-fashioned method of leading by example, by your actions, will count for far more than your words.

Send a verbal or written message and then back it up by consistent non-verbal communication . . . 'walk the talk' and you will not undermine your communication of the purpose.

🌀 THE PAINT IS PEELING OFF THE CEILINGS AND WALLS

I HAD ONLY RECENTLY BEEN APPOINTED TO SOUTH Auckland Health and I was walking about the organisation, meeting staff and gaining an inside perspective on the organisation. I was stunned at the consequences of years and years of deferred maintenance. In the ward bathrooms, there was an unimpressive and frankly depressing cocktail of lack of privacy with see-through shower curtains in mixed-sex bathrooms, peeling paint on the ceilings and walls, chipped basins and baths and the general decay of heavy use unmatched by repairs and maintenance.

I was shocked. The lack of concern for the dignity of staff and patients was palpable. Even worse, this was not a recent problem. For years there were promises of maintenance and refurbishment . . . but nothing ever happened.

Only two or three months before I was appointed, though, the management suite and boardroom had been repainted and redecorated. This had, unsurprisingly, not passed unnoticed by the employees, who were being asked to reduce costs and it impacted adversely on management credibility. Staff were being asked to reduce costs and management was spending on the management suite while the bathrooms were a disgrace.

No matter how understandable this was to management, it was just another case of management's words and actions not being aligned.

You cannot win commitment to purpose or even to short-term objectives if your non-verbal communication, perceived as the most important form of communication, is not aligned to your verbal communication. Employees must be treated with respect and dignity. Communication does need to be both understandable and credible. Organisations and companies fail through

management's undercommunication, which is seen by employees
— and justifiably so — as arrogant inattention.

As a newly appointed chief executive, I was able to use the
bathroom situation as an opportunity to turn a negative into a
positive and begin to refocus employees away from the past and
on to the future.

❦ NOTHING HAPPENS, UNTIL IT HAPPENS

I DECIDED THAT QUITE APART FROM OUR FINANCIAL
situation at the time, the refurbishment of the ward
bathrooms must become an absolute priority. They were a
disgrace and their acceptance, albeit extremely grudgingly
by employees powerless to do anything about it, merely
contributed to a mindset of mediocrity.

If we aspired to greater things we needed a symbol of
development and progress . . . the bathrooms were just that.
This was not a cynical attempt to build support but a
genuine opportunity to achieve a number of objectives,
including:

- providing the appropriate standard bathroom for
  patients and the staff caring for them.
- showing that the organisation was shifting from
  being a passive recipient of a situation, to taking
  control of it.
- showing that decisions could be made rapidly
  without the debilitating bureaucracy.

The decision was made, the relevant employees were
involved in the redesign and refurbishment of the bathrooms
and work on them commenced.

One of my managers came to see me, to tell me that the

charge nurse on one ward did not believe the bathroom in her ward would be done. It was timetabled, she had been involved in the design, she had seen other bathrooms being done . . . but still she was sceptical.

Until the bathroom was done — and it was — she remained disbelieving. She changed only when it was finished, indicating that she now had a more positive view of the future.

I reflected on this situation, which frankly really puzzled me. I realised that the pessimism that resulted from the constant mismatch between what managers say and what managers do (or perhaps more correctly, fail to do) has an effect on individual employees out of all proportion to that which any manager might anticipate. Even worse, that pessimism is transmitted to other employees and can be passed on, in an almost genetic way, from one generation of employees to another.

Speak less, say more . . . and live what you say: your actions speak louder than your words.

PART 3

PLANNING

FIVE

IT SHOULD BE A TELESCOPE, NOT A MICROSCOPE

Great ideas need landing gear as well as wings.

— C. D. Jackson

Understanding where an organisation or company is presently located, and where it aspires to be, is not in itself enough to get it there.

It is important to define direction and inspire a commitment to undertake the journey, but what is needed as well is a roadmap to take the organisation from where it is to where it wishes to be. That roadmap or plan forms the underlying basis of The Whirlpool Effect™ model's second cornerstone, Planning.

Planning is the Siamese twin of purpose, each joined to the other and dependent on the other for survival. Planning and purpose are not simply joined at the hip and able to be separated by simple surgery. Unfortunately in many organisations planning has become an annual procedure rather than a critical ongoing activity. It has become something that 'has to be done' and is often unrelated to action, focusing primarily on the budget. But budget is not a roadmap; it is a forecast of the financial success of the strategic and operational plan.

The unhealthy focus on numbers as the priority in the planning process, together with a highly systematic and absurdly elaborate planning process, has eroded the most important element of planning . . . *thinking*. Thinking is The Whirlpool Effect™ model's first line of leadership related to the cornerstone of Planning.

WHO NEEDS A BRAIN, IT IS ALL ON A DISK

I WAS WORKING FOR A LARGE MULTINATIONAL IN A marketing position and was excitedly looking forward to my first real involvement in the business planning process. I was on the country team to develop the business plan before it was sent to head office for review.

We received a computer disk from head office that included a number of instructions. Having familiarised ourselves with the instructions, we proceeded to review the contents of the disk.

The focus was predominately on sales volumes, pricing, costs and the bottom line. A template was in place and there were vacant cells into which we were to put brief narrative and lots of numbers.

I was taken aback and also disappointed as, freshly armed with an MBA, I was ready for some deep and meaningful development of strategy. However, I could accept that head office set the direction and we should follow it.

We completed the vacant cells on the disk, pressed the appropriate keyboard button to allow the computation to occur — and the bottom line came up ERROR!

We carefully combed the contents of the disk to see what we had done so wrong as to have the fruits of our labour come up as an error. We could not see what we had done incorrectly, so we called head office.

They chuckled and said that the prices we had inserted were below the threshold price in the model and therefore were unacceptable. If we were to put in prices above the threshold, the model would compute appropriately.

I was stunned. Firstly, the threshold prices were invisible, as probably were the thresholds for a range of other numbers. Secondly, we were in a sector where pricing was regulated by government, who were deliberately constraining prices.

We had a number of choices. Put in unachievable numbers above the threshold and get the plan completed, but be unable to deliver on the plan. Put in achievable numbers, but be unable to complete the plan, because the model would not accept them. Create a real plan, with all the elements that implied, a true roadmap to take us from where we were to where we wanted to be.

We called head office again, indicating to them that we were going to pursue the latter course. Big problem: their task was to consolidate all of the countries into a single financial account and if we did not use their disk, how could they do that?

This was an early lesson to me that for many companies, perhaps most companies, planning is an end in itself. A housekeeping procedure, it needs to be done to keep any number of important people happy, and make any number of middle management and employees unhappy. I know this because in spite of my own early experiences, I have made some of these mistakes myself.

Why does modern management do this? Maybe there simply is not time to plan properly . . . once again it is a case of the urgent (the budget) overwhelming the important (the strategy). On second thcughts, perhaps there is time, but that valuable time is wasted on inwardly focused, highly quantitative, historical planning.

In a *Fortune* magazine article dated 31 December 1990, it stated that: 'At too many companies strategic planning has become overly bureaucratic, absurdly quantitative, and largely irrelevant. In executive suites across America, countless five-year plans, updated annually and solemnly in three ring-binders, are gathering dust — their impossible specific prognostications about costs, process and market share long forgotten.'

> **The tool of the leader is the telescope, exploring what lies out in front and using that to provide coordinates for shaping an organisation's future.**

It seems to me that it is unlikely that any organisation or company could capture the future if it itself was a captive of the past. The tool of the modern manager has become the microscope, magnifying the irrelevant and quantifying even that which is realistically unquantifiable. The tool of the leader is the telescope, exploring what lies out in front and using that to provide coordinates for shaping an organisation's future.

Modern management's unhealthy obsession with matters quantitative as the underlying basis of planning has a number of adverse effects. Not the least of these is a discouragement of experimentation and risk-taking, two fundamental building blocks of innovation.

Planning is a means to an end, not an end in itself. While the quantitative element is relevant, the high-level management approach needs to focus as a priority on the qualitative variables.

Possibly the number of chief executives with a strong financial background, particularly in their underlying tertiary education, coupled with the number of chief executives who are weak on finance and dependent on their chief financial officer, who is therefore often the driver of the planning process in any event, is the problem. Whatever the underlying reason, we need to move away from the simplistic planning model of extrapolating historical numbers. This is the type of robotic planning that occurs in too many organisations and does nothing to influence what actually happens in the organisation over the ensuing year or years.

We need to move to a planning model which has an emphasis on thinking and on The Whirlpool Effect™ model's second line of leadership, *judgment*.

❧ SITTING IN JUDGMENT ON JUDGMENT

I BET IF YOU ASKED A GROUP OF MANAGERS WHETHER GOOD judgment was a critical management and leadership attribute, they would all say yes. Furthermore, if you put the proposition to them that good judgment came from experience, most and probably all would agree with you.

If it is true that good judgment is important, and that it results from experience, then where does experience come from?

Experience comes from bad judgment! More on this over the page.

Judgment is clearly an attribute that develops as a result of both formal and informal learning, being exposed to a variety of situations, making mistakes and learning from them. But judgment is also a personal quality that allows certain individuals to have an immense and powerful ability to reason, to analyse and to utilise an instinctive 'feel'. Some of these latter elements can never be learnt, but like strength, speed or agility in a champion athlete, there are leaders who have these qualities in abundance.

John Wareham has described judgment as 'A higher order of skill than mere reasoning, the infinitely more refined capacity of considering an ambiguous situation, and using both logic and intuition to make a really good guess.'

Judgment is a quality of the neck-top computer, not the lap-top computer. Human beings do have a role in thinking and planning way beyond that of the computer. That is because planning, the application of thinking and judgment, is an exercise of strategy . . . not in spreadsheeting. The spreadsheet merely performs arithmetic gymnastics on the numerical results of the thinking and the judgment.

❧ THE TEST FIRST AND THE LESSON AFTERWARDS

I ONCE HEARD THIS STORY ABOUT A MARKETING EXECUTIVE in a major toy company. She was a charismatic, talented and energetic person with extremely strong powers of persuasion.

Against almost everybody's will she managed to launch a new product, which unfortunately was a rapid and complete failure, costing the company $15 million.

Her boss felt that he should fire her, but first consulted his boss, who agreed but decided to check it out with her boss . . . the chief executive.

The chief executive on hearing the story, reflected for a few moments and then said: 'Why would we fire somebody, when we have just invested $15 million into their education?'

Thinking is the bridge linking purpose and planning. Thinking assists in carefully and clearly defining the purpose and direction of the organisation or company. It is important that both purpose and direction are clear as they will become the litmus test for operational decisions that are then accepted or rejected.

The thinking process creates the beachhead for both strategic and operational planning and shifts the whole mindset from an incremental calendar of events to an intellectual and challenging process focused strongly on experimentation.

A mindset of experimentation as part of planning is important to extinguish the rigidity that most planning processes in organisations and companies tend to have. Experimentation, in my view, will also serve as a constant reminder to managers that planning is an ongoing, live and dynamic process. Planning helps breathe life into the organisation or company, rather than managers breathing life into the planning process for a few months each year.

Managers sitting around a room with a whiteboard is an unlikely scenario for anticipating consequences. Experimentation can actually provide lessons, real lessons that cannot be learnt leaning on the whiteboard, felt-tip pen in hand. This is not to say that experimentation replaces planning, but that it should become part of the mix. As a consequence I have selected *experimentation* as the third line of leadership for The Whirlpool Effect™ model's cornerstone of planning.

Experimentation is a key driver of innovation which in itself comprises a purposeful exploration for a change that results in something different or something new. Most innovation is not necessarily something new but rather something that capitalises on change — minor, moderate or major.

Where does innovation start? In sensing opportunity, is my guess. Innovation germinates from focus and from simplicity and tends to be evolutionary. More than anything else, innovation depends on experimentation and risk-taking, which themselves depend totally on leadership.

When planning — particularly when experimenting and taking risks — it is important that any changes that are made add and do not destroy value. This is a lesson that most managers should learn, but many do not. The reason for this is that they are so remote from the consequences of their decisions that they do not see, feel, smell, taste or touch the impacts. Without some sensory perception of the impact, how can you learn?

It strikes me that a lot of managers seem to think that the purpose of planning is to produce plans. It is emphatically not — the purpose of planning, simply, is to produce results. Not mediocre results, not meeting tame targets, but bold and outrageous results: results that show the organisation or company is delivering to its potential.

As important as thinking, judgment and experimentation are to planning, in themselves they are insufficient to truly deliver on the organisation's or company's potential. To do this requires the fourth line of leadership in The Whirlpool Effect™ model's cornerstone of Planning . . . *creativity*.

The *Oxford Dictionary* defines 'creativity' as inventive or imaginative. John Wareham defines creativity in a manner much more meaningful in an organisational context as '. . . judgment plus imagination. It is the capacity to imagine and process data, make new connections, and come up with fresh ideas and solutions.'

Unfortunately, creativity is something that you are born with rather than something that you can develop as a skill. It is spoken of a lot in the entertainment and advertising business, but is not something necessarily associated with management, and rarely linked with planning.

Creativity does include creative imitation, of which the Japanese are a good example. For a long time they have focused on imitating and adapting with astonishing success. They developed the ability to understand what the underlying innovation represented better than the people who actually thought of it in the first place.

Obviously creativity also includes something that is completely and utterly new.

In the planning process, creativity across the spectrum from imitation to true innovation is important and should form the critical element of the planning. With the purpose in place, planning must begin at the strategic level. Frequently, this critical part of the plan, the strategic plan, is neglected or paid insufficient attention. The reason for this is that in the planning process, the strategic and operational planning are often not separated, or due to pressure of time, the operational planning (more particularly the budgeting) begins before the strategic plan.

This is often compounded in larger organisations. I know this because I have made these mistakes myself. If the strategic plan and the operational plans are not separated in the planning process, it is extremely likely that the urgency of operational issues will dominate.

The strategic plan, as I see it, defines and clarifies purpose and medium- to longer-term direction. The operational plan is focused on implementation and the short-term direction. It is the operational plan that provides the 'landing gear' for great ideas, which form part of the strategic plan.

Both strategic and operational plans contain qualitative as well as quantitative information and need to be backed up by a performance management plan, which allows management to compare actual performance (both qualitative and quantitative) with that forecast in strategic and operational plans.

> **There needs to be careful and thoughtful linkages between purpose, strategic plan, operational plan and performance management plan.**

There needs to be careful and thoughtful linkages between purpose, strategic plan, operational plan and performance management plan. Minor disconnections can derail the organisation or company, just as a small piece of broken rail can derail a train, independent of the fact that hundreds of kilometres of rail before that point were perfectly linked.

Linkage is the fifth line of leadership in The Whirlpool Effect™ model's cornerstone of Planning.

Plans do relate to purpose in that despite the most intricate and technical planning, employees at all levels, including line management, will not implement what they do not understand and are not committed to.

All the best thinking, judgment, experimentation, creativity and linkage will bear no fruit if the plan is developed without real, meaningful and active participation of employees, at all levels and undertaking all functions. This goes beyond communication, extending to formal involvement of employees right throughout the planning process. Not token inclusion, but active participation allowing debate, disagreement and real opportunity to assist in shaping the future.

> **All the best thinking, judgment, experimentation, creativity and linkage will bear no fruit if the plan is developed without real, meaningful and active participation of all employees, at all levels and undertaking all functions.**

Participation is the final line of leadership in The Whirlpool Effect™ model's cornerstone of Planning.

This level of participation is difficult to manage and is time-consuming. Plans, like purpose, need to reside in the heart and not only the head. Participation also requires the candid sharing of information that many organisations and companies possibly regard as commercially sensitive.

The type of organisational climate proposed does require high levels of trust.

SIX

IF YOU CAN MEASURE IT, YOU MAY UNDERSTAND IT

In the long run men hit only what they aim at.

— Henry David Thoreau

If you carefully dissect the average business plan you may have difficulty in differentiating between the strategic plan, the operational plan and performance management plan. Even when the differences are clear, the linkages are often missing or confused.

❧ A JOURNEY OF DISCOVERY . . . I THINK

There is a lovely story about Christopher Columbus.
When he left, he did not know where he was going.
When he got there, he did not know where he was.
When he got back, he did not know where he had been.
And he did all of this with somebody else's money!

As tongue in cheek as this may be, it represents a situation that frequently occurs within organisations and companies.

Planning needs to be undertaken in a careful and measured way, so that it becomes a reference document, as important to managers and employees as navigation charts on a ship.

Planning needs to be undertaken in a careful and measured way, so that it becomes a reference document, as important to managers and employees as navigation charts on a ship. A good plan is referred to constantly to ensure that the organisation or company is travelling to the coordinates laid down.

Most managers would agree that the strategic plan is broad and conceptual in nature. Where there does not seem to be agreement is in relation to the contents. I do not believe that the shape and form of the strategic plan needs to be universally prescriptive. What is important, in my view, is that whatever shape and form is chosen by an organisation or company, there needs to be consistency.

If the shape and form of the plan changes significantly each year, it causes unnecessary confusion and makes relevant comparisons difficult. The words 'keep it simple' are often spoken in relation to planning, but when the planning begins the process invariably becomes irreparably complex.

The strategic plan needs to be clear, simple and easily understood. The shape and form that I prefer, and that in my experience is easily understood and practical in its use, comprises four specific components:

PURPOSE

As I have discussed previously, the purpose identifies the direction of travel and the destination for the organisation or company. It states the underlying philosophy of the organisation or company, the reason that it exists. All other elements of the strategic plan and the operational plan are obliged to be in direct support of the purpose.

Like most things, this is easier said than done. Firstly, the purpose needs to be sufficiently well defined in order that the other elements of the plan link directly into it. Secondly, it is not possible for all the elements to link to the purpose directly. Many will link indirectly, and it is the indirect linkages that are more likely to fail to connect.

The purpose fundamentally addresses the 'what' questions.

THE STRATEGIC DATABASE

This is the underlying analysis of all factors which will impinge directly or indirectly on the company's activities, now or in the future, definitely or possibly, locally or globally, affecting markets or products, including factors that are regulatory or competitive in relation to the organisation or company.

This analysis is critical as it assists in the process of thinking, judgment, experimentation and creativity and allows the most relevant, coherent and robust assumptions to be made.

I regard assumptions as the most important part of the strategic planning process. When you are looking into the future, you are compelled to make assumptions. As time unfolds, you are able to adjust your plan to take account of how your forecast of events meets reality. This is where exceptional judgment separates winners from also-rans and losers.

The assumptions that evolve from the strategic database, in my view form the anchor of the planning process and plan, preventing it from drifting aimlessly.

The analytical process assists in identifying the critical issues that the organisation or company will face, and helps weight these, so that they attract appropriate resources and emphasis. The development of the strategic database is an ongoing exercise which must continue independent of planning cycles. The strategic database addresses the 'why' question and its key outputs are the assumptions and critical issues.

STRATEGIC GOALS

I identify strategic goals as the organisation's or company's broadly defined aims that link directly into the purpose. To reach its potential and maintain focus, in my experience an organisation or company should select fewer, rather than more strategic goals.

When caught up in the excitement of the planning, there is always the temptation to select so many goals as to make the process unrealistic and even meaningless. I recommend three to five strategic goals that when achieved will take the organisation either to its destination or very close to it. These strategic goals must be measurable and fundamentally address the 'where' question.

Strategic goals generally will have a timeframe of five to ten years.

 ### ISN'T TEN YEARS A LONG TIME?

MY EXPERIENCE HAS BEEN TO PLAN AT LEAST TEN YEARS INTO the future. The most common question I was asked about my long-range planning was, isn't ten years a long time?

I used to try to explain that while we did develop a ten-year plan, my own thinking was twenty-five to thirty years into the future. At this point the listener's eyes would glaze over and they would either feign interest or politely excuse themselves.

One day while travelling in an airplane and flicking through a magazine to pass the time, I read about a

Japanese chief executive of one of the major companies. When asked the question about his frame on long-term planning, he simply answered, 'One hundred years.'

When the interviewing journalist asked him what one most needed to have as an attribute for planning over such a long-term horizon, he simply answered, 'Patience.'

The reason modern management struggles with true long-term planning is because they are self-focused. They find it difficult to think beyond the point when they are no longer there or even alive, as if the company's future is utterly and totally dependent only on them.

I do not think that the modern practice of placing senior executives — or indeed managers at any level — on short-term contracts actually assists. I am uncertain as to the value of such contracts; if they are a mechanism to address inadequate performance, there needs to be a better way. My experience is that if you put somebody on a three-year contract they are very likely to think on a three-year timeframe and to position the organisation or company, the department, the product or service in the way that best creates a platform for their next position.

LONG-TERM OBJECTIVES

Long-term objectives identify what the organisation or company wants to have achieved at some clearly defined point in the future. I have generally worked with long-term objectives as having a three-year timeframe.

Long-term objectives must be measurable and they address the 'how' and 'when' questions. Like strategic goals, they need to be well defined and very clear and again it is important that the number is restricted to somewhere between four and six.

The long-term objectives are obliged to link directly into the achievement of the strategic goals.

FINANCIAL MODELS

The strategic plan should contain a ten-year financial model. All financial information that is relevant is presented in the model and is supportive of the achievement of long-term objectives, strategic goals and purpose.

Following the completion of the strategic plan, the operational plan needs to be developed. In my experience, the operational plan is the action plan. It is the detailed tactical roadmap, focused on a one-year timeframe.

The operational plan needs to be highly specific and detailed. I have tended to favour the following shape and form:

- **OPERATIONAL DATABASE**

  The operational analysis will reveal a database far more specific and detailed than the strategic database. It will identify a set of assumptions that over the year that unfolds should be reasonably closely aligned to what actually occurs. Again, as with the strategic database, it will identify the critical issues which form a platform for the development of the short-term objectives.

  The operational database addresses the 'why' question.

- **SHORT-TERM OBJECTIVES**

  These objectives have a one-year timeframe and are tightly measurable and need to link directly into the achievement of longer-term objectives and strategic goals.

  There is a very specific emphasis on how the organisation or company is moving forward over the forthcoming year and the main purpose of this plan is to achieve the results outlined in the first year of the strategic plan.

The short-term objectives must be supported by an action plan that ensures their translation into results. Short-term objectives address very specifically the 'how' and 'when' questions.

Short-term objectives should preferably number no more than ten and should clearly identify what the result is, the timetable for its achievement, the resources it will require and who carries full responsibility for the achievement.

- **CRITICAL PERFORMANCE INDICATORS**

For any planning process to be successful, the important indicators of performance need to be identified and measured.

I do not subscribe to the modern management madness that espouses the theory, 'if you can't measure it, you can't manage it.' This is typical of the modern manager and their microscope. Measurement is important, but it needs to be viewed in a wider perspective than simply to quantify. It is also a way to qualify.

My view is that if you can measure it, it will help you understand it; if you understand it, it will help you manage it. I think leaders tend to worry more about what to measure than about how to measure it.

I often hear managers saying they need more information, more data, more numbers, more ratios, more analysis. I actually think we need less information — what we need is more *relevant* information.

> **I actually think we need less information — what we need is more *relevant* information.**

The measures we require are those that are critical to our decision-making and judgment. You will notice I have used the term 'critical performance indicators' as opposed to the more commonly used 'key performance indicators'.

In my experience, the collection of performance indicators has become partially trivialised and I am trying to place an emphasis on collecting only that information which is important in determining whether the organisation or company is performing to its potential.

Modern managers tend to isolate rather than correlate variables. The correlation is important to develop a total picture of performance before making a decision to take some specific line of action.

- **BUDGETS**

Finally, we've got to it . . . the famous budget! You will see that in my framework it is the last element to fall in place and occurs as a result of completing the strategic plan and the other elements of the operational plan.

Why is it that this subservient element seems to be able to so dominate the process of planning in so many organisations and companies? The reason is that modern management does not have a truly visible and powerful commitment to purpose and strategy. This is why so many organisations and companies are in difficulty, or are under-performing.

Exceptional planning requires exceptional leadership as well as a clearly defined process that is highly participative. If the first meeting with an employee group focuses entirely on next year's budget, do not expect significant innovation.

Something that I learned early on is not to let the financial manager highjack the planning process. Their role is to manage the financial model and budget compilation and that is where their focus needs to be.

To ensure that strategic and operational planning is relevant, it is important to create a performance management plan which is basically a mechanism to monitor the success or otherwise of the implementation of the strategic and operational plan. This plan identifies the strategic goals, long-term objectives, short-term objectives, critical performance indicators and critical elements from the financial model and operational budget.

> To ensure that strategic and operational planning is relevant, it is important to create a performance management plan which is basically a mechanism to monitor the success or otherwise of the implementation of the strategic and operational plan.

It identifies the forecast result and at predetermined times measures that against the actual result, focusing carefully on ensuring linkage between objectives, goals and purpose in order to determine progress . . . this, after all, is the reason we have plans at all.

PART 4
PROCESS

SEVEN | PRICE, QUALITY, SPEED, CHOOSE ANY TWO

If you don't do it excellently, don't do it at all.

— Robert Townsend

The third cornerstone of The Whirlpool Effect™ model is Process, which is generally defined as a collection of activities that takes any number and type of input and creates an output that is of value to the customer.

I like to use the word 'process' in preference to 'structure' and 'systems' as the latter words convey an imagery of functional silos or vertical structures, where employees look inward, not to their organisation or company, but to the smallest functional sub-unit, their department or a component of it. These employees look upwards towards their manager with almost no one looking outwards towards the customer . . . in other words bureaucracy.

This is because managers and employees are generally focused on *tasks*, working within structures and systems. They are not generally focused on process. If you wish to have this confirmed to you, try being a customer!

LEADERSHIP AND THE WHIRLPOOL EFFECT™

🍂 FLICK OF THE WRIST

I HAD BEEN IN MY JOB AS CHIEF EXECUTIVE OF SOUTH Auckland Health only for a few days when my assistant asked me to take a call from a very upset close relative of a patient.

I spoke to the relative and asked her to carefully explain what the problem was. She did this and after having a quick look at the time on my wristwatch (it was 3.30 pm), I told her to leave it with me and that I would solve it and call her back within the hour.

She was satisfied with that. I then called the manager of the relevant department, told them what the problem was and asked for them to give me a call within 30 minutes with the outcome.

At 4.20 pm, ten minutes before I was due to call the relative, I had still not heard back from the manager. I called him again and he explained that he had asked the operations manager, who reported to him, to check it out. He had not heard back from the operations manager.

Now feeling mildly frustrated myself, I suggested to him that I would speak directly to the operations manager. I called the operations manager, but he was not at his desk. I rang the switchboard and asked them to page him.

I had heard nothing back at 4.31 pm, so I felt compelled to call the relative as promised. I explained that I was on to the case, but that I had not yet been able to solve the problem, and would they mind if I called at 5.30 pm.

She seemed pleased that someone was interested and left me to it. By 4.45 pm I had heard nothing and being very concerned about 5.00 pm approaching and everyone disappearing exactly on time, I decided to head down to that department.

There is a story told by David Ogilvy about what he calls 'Peculiar Behaviour'. He talks about being astonished by working habits that differed from his own. Once, while discussing a copywriter at another agency, whose abilities he somewhat admired, he said, 'Listen to this — every day at precisely five o'clock that man gets up from his desk, puts on his hat and his coat, and goes home.' Then, leaning forward for emphasis, Ogilvy added, 'Think of the extraordinary self-discipline that requires!' I myself experienced this day in and day out, as there was a department on the floor below my office which finished at 4.30 pm. At exactly 4.25 pm each day there would be the ritual banging shut of windows, an amazing self-discipline in action.

Anyhow, anxious to beat the self-disciplined, I rushed up to find the operations manager. He was in his office packing his bag at 4.55 pm. I raised the problem with him and he said he had passed it on to the relevant charge nurse. I dashed to the ward to find the charge nurse, who explained to me, as he said he had explained to the operations manager, that although the problem was related to his patient, it was an issue that occurred in another department.

You guessed it — the problem had been passed to the other department, a clinical support service. I ran at high speed to that department, but the relevant person was gone. Bright idea! I contacted the afternoon duty manager, sure that they would have left the problem with her to solve. But no, no one had mentioned anything to her; they left the problem on their desk, the relative, patient and me all irrelevant.

I went back to my office and called the relative. I told

her what I was going through and that it seemed unlikely that I could solve the problem until the next day. She sympathised because she had been through a similar process. She said she felt sorry for me, because at least she could complain to me, who could I complain to?

The next morning I went through a maze of people, the problem being flicked from one functional unit to another, from one vertical silo to another, with no one apparently able to solve it. I had had enough. Here I was as chief executive with total authority, unable to get to the bottom of a simple issue. Boy, did I feel sorry for the relative! They had no authority at all.

I called an immediate conference of all the parties. Once together they had no excuse other than to solve the problem together. They did this in a matter of minutes. What shocked me is that they did not have the interest or ability to work outside their structure and system — they did not care about the process at all. Because it was an organisation with functional divisions and a hierarchy, they shifted the problem from one silo to another and downwards within a silo. With a flick of a wrist, from person to person, down the hierarchy until it lands up on the desk of someone without the time or authority to actually solve it.

This true story emphasises how individual tasks within any process are important, but none really matters to the customer if the overall process does not work. The classical business structure that I have described tends to fragment processes, stifling service and creating a lack of responsiveness.

Coordination is the first line of leadership in The Whirlpool Effect™ model's cornerstone of Process.

In casual conversation, unifying fragmented business tasks into a seamless process makes immediate sense to almost everyone, especially customers. The reality is that in organisations and companies with a tradition focused on structure and systems, built around fragmented basic tasks, the real development of coordination is a major challenge.

The reality is that in organisations and companies with a tradition focused on structure and systems, built around fragmented basic tasks, the real development of coordination is a major challenge.

Organisational structure and tight job descriptions create a 'straight-jacket', rendering an organisation or company inflexible. It introduces a customer-unfriendly rigidity and a mindset amongst individual employees that they are responsible only for their part of the process and not the collective whole.

Organisations and companies with traditional structures and systems do not encourage any particular individual to 'own' the customer. I think that modern organisations and companies need to cast off the practices of the past and confront the fact that the traditional way of doing business no longer works. This is largely because of the impact of the power of the customer and competition as a result of globalisation, innovation and niche marketing.

If customers do hold the upper hand, how come service is still so bad? It is because modern management is not flexible enough and quick enough to change, to keep pace with the way customers' demands and needs have altered.

I have often been unimpressed when managers incessantly bleat for more resources, particularly in the public sector, when what they really need is more coordination. I believe that coordination

I have often been unimpressed when managers incessantly bleat for more resources, particularly in the public sector, when what they really need is more coordination.

really only occurs in the best possible way when there is teamwork in place. Traditional organisational structures do not in themselves necessarily stimulate or encourage teamwork. In many ways traditional organisational structures, by forcing competition for resources between departments, almost actively discourage teamwork and prevent the opportunity of seeing the organisation as a whole, rather than a functional sub-unit. The traditional structure tends to reinforce patch-protection and empire-building within discrete functional areas becomes an art form.

Ultimately, the performance of any organisation depends on each individual's excellence and also on how they work together. By working as a team, a combination of individuals becomes much more effective and will assist in the organisation or company meeting its potential. Teamwork has also become essential because no single manager or employee can have the credibility, time and information to make and implement major decisions all of the time.

Teamwork is often confused with friendship and 'getting along'. That would be nice as a bonus but it is not essential.

Fundamentally, teamwork is about harnessing energy which results from a common sense of purpose. In teams, individuals work together in a complementary way, independent of whether they are working within a function or across functions. The focus is on the development of a process that allows the team to provide for the needs of the customer in the best possible manner. Teamwork requires individuals to put aside their selfish needs, desires and concerns and to focus on commonality . . . on what is good for the organisation or company and the customer.

Teamwork is often rejected by individuals because they feel that it compromises their autonomy. This is more common with professionals, but it need not be so. Exceptional teamwork can actually promote autonomy . . . paradoxical as it sounds.

Teamwork requires a blend of leading and following. The leader will not always be the same person, depending on the outcome required. Teamwork actually requires much more flexibility and role reconfiguration than most people realise.

Teamwork is highly dependent on trust between all individuals concerned. I shall deal with trust later in part 5.

✿ ROW, ROW, ROW YOUR BOAT

I CANNOT REMEMBER WHERE I READ THIS STORY, BUT IT IS an excellent one.

Have you ever watched a rowing eight in action?

It is an amazing sight, eight strong rowers seated one behind the other with a small coxswain at one end of the boat. The first thing you notice is that none of the rowers are facing in the direction that they are rowing! The only person facing the direction that they are moving towards is the coxswain.

It all looks so odd, these big powerful rowers not looking where they are going, totally dependent on the coxswain for direction and on a rower calling the stroke, who determines the pace. In fact, it looks like a bad management model. Quite to the contrary, it is a brilliant example of teamwork and of real trust.

The rowers have absolute trust in the judgment of the coxswain and the stroke. Each rower has their ability and contributes their part to the collective speed of the boat. Each oar in perfect synchrony, no one individual seeking attention, the focus is on the group as if it were one.

If there is trust and practice — and teamwork in organisations and companies is very dependent on practice — there can be teamwork. It is possible to be like a rower and not even look where you are going, because steering happens to be someone else's role.

Imagine if rower five decided to row at a different pace, or if rower three decided to face in the opposite direction, or if rower six decided to only stroke every minute . . . There would be no teamwork and the crew would underperform.

Simple, isn't it?

Teamwork is the second line of leadership of The Whirlpool Effect™ model's cornerstone of Process.

Teams are not committees. The difference between a team and a committee is that a team has a common agenda, whereas committees have separate agendas.

Teamwork and coordination, in large measure, can cut the umbilical cord that modern management has with traditional organisational structure. They make a statement about how managers relate to employees, how managers relate to managers, how employees relate to managers, how employees relate to employees . . . but most of all, how the organisation or company relates to its customers.

Traditional organisational structures make the unhealthy assumption that a one-dimensional organisational chart on a piece of paper can be translated into something meaningful in a dynamic, three-dimensional organisation or company. Traditional organisational structures depend conceptually on the organisation being a hierarchy.

Everyone in an organisation needs to understand their role, who they report to, which team they belong to. However, the assumption cannot be made that these will all be static . . . they can, they will and they should change, depending on changing circumstances.

> **Teamwork and coordination create a sense of community, which gives a sense of equal worth to all members and creates a climate for sharing.**

Traditional functional structures are not an encouraging climate for devolution. Teamwork and coordination create a sense of community, which gives a sense of equal worth to all members and creates a climate for sharing. This is a much more liberating environment, one which fosters innovation.

I sense that it is not possible to contemplate the subject of process, without mentioning BPR — 'business process re-engineering', technobabble at its best. Simplistically, many organisations and companies use process re-engineering in the hope that it can assist them to overcome short-term problems and particularly, reduce costs. High-priced consultants in well-pressed blue suits will rightly tell you that process re-engineering is the 'fundamental rethinking and radical redesign of business process to achieve dramatic improvements in critical contemporary measures of performance, such as cost, quality and speed'. If asked to identify the four key words in this definition, they would point to *fundamental*, *radical*, *dramatic* and *process*.

❧ PRICE, QUALITY, SPEED

I WAS ONCE TOLD BY SOMEONE I KNEW THE FOLLOWING STORY.

When he was at an overseas conference he was staying in a budget hotel in the commercial part of town. He was trying to sleep, but was constantly distracted by a flicking neon light shining into his room.

He got out of bed to attempt to block the light. However the curtains were too flimsy. So rather than try to sleep again, he opened the window to enjoy the evening air.

He looked across at the wretched neon sign, a very large sign in four colours. The sign was above a print shop and it said . . .

TRIPLE X PRINT SHOP
Price
Quality
Speed
CHOOSE ANY TWO

The problem with process re-engineering is that it is most often perceived by employees as a strategic-sounding way to cut costs. Their first response will generally be that quality will deteriorate, based on the traditional view that many employees hold, namely the more you spend on something, the better the quality.

Coherently implemented, process re-engineering does not focus primarily on cutting costs. It focuses on process redesign to improve quality, a result of which is that costs may be reduced, remain the same, or indeed increase. However in most traditionally structured organisations, process redesign will usually improve quality and reduce costs. This is due to streamlining activities, removing bottlenecks and involving as few people as possible in each process.

The outcome in any case is likely to be that jobs are lost. This is a major reason for the cynical way in which employees continue to view process re-engineering. The only real option for managers is to ensure any process re-engineering is aligned to the shared purpose, has resulted from a participative planning process and has objectives which are honestly and clearly stated up-front.

Modern management, when addressing process, loves to talk about efficiency. This is a particular favourite of high-ranking officials in government departments. It has long been my view that efficiency cannot be dealt with in isolation. If efficiency is defined as *resource utilisation*, then to be coherent, it needs another arm. Otherwise, it merely becomes 'doing things right', and in itself will not promote achievement of potential for an organisation or company.

The other arm of efficiency is effectiveness, otherwise defined as *goal achievement*. Effectiveness is regarded as 'doing the right thing'. The net result of efficiency and effectiveness is productivity, which is achieving a company's objectives, goals and purpose while using all its resources in the most appropriate way. These resources may include human resources, financial resources, plant and equipment, technology, information and time.

> An inappropriate emphasis on efficiency may not lead to any improvement or progress towards potential at all.

Productivity is the third line of leadership in The Whirlpool Effect™ model's cornerstone of Process. Productivity becomes understandable to employees when it links the use of resources to the achievement of objectives, goals and purpose.

It is important to effect a balance between efficiency and

effectiveness, something that in many organisations and companies does not occur. An inappropriate emphasis on efficiency may not lead to any improvement or progress towards potential at all.

❧ IS IT TYPEWRITING OR WORD PROCESSING?

ONE ESSENTIAL ELEMENT OF KEYBOARDS HAS REMAINED unchanged since the first Remington typewriter — the arrangement of the keys, nicknamed QWERTY for the top line of letters, was designed to make it easier for the salesmen touting the machines to their clients to demonstrate their capabilities.

Since every letter in the (then revolutionary) word 'typewriter' was in the top line of the keyboard, the salesman could give the impression of efficiency by banging out the word without having to 'hunt and peck' over the whole keyboard. While there is no doubt that this configuration of letters on the keyboard still works, its initial rationale is now lost in the mists of time.

A vastly more efficient arrangement was devised in 1936 by August Dvorak, cousin of the famous composer (keyboards obviously ran in the family!). On this particular keyboard, the right hand did equal work with the left hand and the strongest fingers did most of the typing. Furthermore, 70 percent of the typing took place on the 'home' row where the fingers naturally rest.

It is strange, then, that the QWERTY keyboard still remains the standard for word processors, when the rest of the machine has undergone such revolutionary changes with the 'electronic revolution'. The only real justification for retaining it is that of familiarity, since the original rationale (salesmen who are two-finger typists) no longer exists. It is even possible that the Dvorak keyboard would go a long way towards reducing occupational stress, since its configuration is that much more operator-friendly.

So why does the original keyboard remain when the circumstances that gave rise to it have changed?

The real reasons, I suggest, are:

- lazy minds transferring the status quo from one generation to the next.
- a mindset which says, 'If it ain't broke, why fix it?'

The danger of this approach is being stuck with solutions to a problem which while arguably 'efficient' have long since outgrown their effectiveness in terms of contribution to a desired outcome.

Effective teams, elegantly coordinated and guided by an inspiring, shared purpose, supported by coherent plans, will inevitably deliver exceptional productivity.

Where disconnection occurs between managers and employees, managers often talk productivity but mean efficiency, or even tactical, short-term cost reduction.

EIGHT | **GOOD IS NOT ENOUGH, WHEN YOU DREAM OF BEING GREAT**

There aren't any rules here, we are trying to get something done.

— Thomas Edison

To reach their productivity potential, organisations and companies increasingly need to build on the advantage of recent advances in technology.

Unfortunately the ability of far too many organisations to take advantage of contemporary and emerging technology lags way behind the available opportunities. The major reason for this, in my experience, is that technology is too frequently seen as playing a supportive role, rather than a strategic one.

Cast in a supportive role, technology will tend to promote short-term efficiency rather than longer-term productivity. To gain clarity on the role of technology requires the modern manager to look through the telescope not down the microscope. Technology has the potential to transform the nature of an organisation's products or services, even their markets.

The financial services industry is a classic example where

technology has erased conventional market limitations, through the introduction of automatic-teller machines, electronic banking and internet banking.

✿ MAYBE BANKS ADOPTED NEW TECHNOLOGY BECAUSE THEY HAD TO?

A FRIEND OF MINE IN THE STATES TELLS THIS GREAT STORY about his bank.

One day, while driving in his car, he heard a radio commercial advertising his bank. The thrust of the commercial was that the bank would deposit $50 into any customer's bank account if that customer received bad service.

He was amazed to hear this because his bank provided such consistently bad service that if he went in and out of the bank doing transactions for a day, he would stand to make a lot of money.

Unfortunately he was called out of town on business before he had a chance to visit the bank.

On his return, he rushed into the bank and did a transaction. The teller rudely flung his receipt on the counter, loudly calling, 'Next!'

My friend said, 'Slow down, before you attend to the next customer, please deposit $50 into my account.'

The teller rudely asked why. My friend explained that he had heard the commercial and had been called out of town. Now that he had returned, had done his transaction and had been treated rudely, he wanted the promised $50.

The teller laughed and laughed, with my friend growing increasingly impatient. When the teller finally gained control of himself, my friend asked what was so funny.

The teller responded, 'That promotion ended on Friday.'

Enabling technology is the fourth line of leadership in The Whirlpool Effect™ model's cornerstone of Process. I view enabling technology as any form of technology that plays a transforma-tional role, rather than an infrastructural role. Enabling

I view enabling technology as any form of technology that plays a transformational role, rather than an infrastructural role.

technology has the power to change an industry by refining it and altering its level of sophistication. Those managers whose perspective on technology is not strategic are already being adversely affected by technology-based substitution — the eclipse of postal carriers by electronic mail is a simple and current example.

A non-strategic view of enabling technology will also be blind to changes affecting entry barriers into your industry or markets, particularly those neutralising or eliminating them. If entry barriers are lowered, new entrants will generally enter the most profitable niches of the market, reshaping that market's competitive forces.

It is important that technology adds true value, rather than simply adding cost. Introduction of technology in sectors and markets with insufficient price elasticity is often seen to be impossible, but companies in such areas are often those that need it most.

While enabling technology can create vitality for your organisation or company, assisting in the journey towards excellence, the non-strategic implementation of technology may undo more than it achieves. Technology is not automation; rather it is an enabler, creating new opportunities to reconfigure processes. More often than not, the modern manager by miscasting technology has tended to reinforce old ways of

> More often than not, the modern manager by miscasting technology has tended to reinforce old ways of thinking rather than creating new ones.

thinking rather than creating new ones. This kind of perspective on technology is frighteningly common and adds significant cost but no value — very often value is subtracted.

The adoption and application of enabling technologies should allow our organisations and companies to do a 'Bob Beamon' — to go places no one has been before. Emerging technologies in particular, contain latent possibilities. The exceptional thinker, the leader who has intellect and imagination, will see the opportunity to apply emerging technology to create outcomes not yet thought possible. To think in this way almost always requires rules to be broken, to expose an opportunity locked away behind layers of bureaucracy and unwieldy organisational structures.

It is interesting to reflect that enabling technology, particularly information technology, liberates information necessary for decision-making. This allows employees at the 'coal-face' to make immediate decisions without reference to their line managers. Employees love this new freedom, as do customers. But not all managers are enamoured of it, because to eliminate hierarchical decision-making is to eliminate the need for many line managers!

I have been amazed by the traditional thinking that is applied to the development of buildings, particularly where technology is already reframing service delivery. As Winston Churchill said, 'We shape our buildings, and then they shape us.' Health is a classic example and one of which I have reasonable experience. Yet healthcare facilities are so frequently cast for a time now past. The more equipment- and capital-intensive a service operation is — and hospitals fall squarely within this range — then the more likely it is that the effective use of physical resources will impact on the ability to provide exceptional service. Dull management, captured in the past, will seldom be alert to identifying technologies which are not traditionally in the orbit of that industry or are still emerging but which may have the ability to transform an organisation or company and allow it to meet its potential.

Desperate management facing difficult circumstances should not however think they can merely pull the enabling technology lever and their problems will disappear. No technology application will rescue a poorly led organisation or company. An integrated, well-thought-through strategic application of enabling techno-logy can enhance quality, reduce or rationalise costs and by affecting employees in a positive way, bring your organisation or company closer to the customer.

> **Clumsy or crude technology application, particularly in service industries, might reduce or rationalise costs but could also create a major disruption in the relationship customers have with your organisation and with your employees.**

Clumsy or crude technology application, particularly in service industries, might reduce or rationalise costs but could also create a major disruption in the relationship customers have with your organisation and with your employees. This is dangerous territory and reduces entry barriers to those operators who are more sensitive to the social needs of customers.

If purpose sets the destination and direction while planning

> **You can talk about quality programmes, undertake quality training, appoint quality assurance officers . . . but until you become customer-focused, it is all a real waste.**

creates the roadmap, process defines a framework for achieving the journey. Most managers do not see process — they see structures and systems, things to be erected and controlled. Despite this they all talk convincingly about quality as if it is a systems issue. But like almost everything else that propels an organisation towards or away from its potential, quality is linked to process and is a people issue.

It is not possible to be a quality organisation or company if your focus is internal. You can talk about quality programmes, undertake quality training, appoint quality assurance officers . . . but until you become customer-focused, it is all a real waste. If management has a problem listening to its employees, it also has one in hearing what its customers say. It is not possible to build a quality franchise in this type of environment. To improve quality, the painful and difficult changes need to be first made by senior management.

One of the issues facing management in the quality debate is their ability to disrupt their own thinking about continuity, or to put it more bluntly, to break long-standing roles. Management is happy to disrupt the continuity, whether appropriately or inappropriately, of its employees, but seldom its own.

❧ THERE IS MORE TO LIFE THAN A SORE BOTTOM

THE AUTHOR OF *FUTURE EDGE*, JOEL BARKER, TALKS OF shifting established mindsets and changing what has come to pass as the accepted model.

He raises the issue of bicycle seats and suggests it would be better riding a bicycle with a comfortable seat, one which is much wider and more flexible than the traditional seat.

He suggests that a bicycle seat was originally made to look like a horse saddle — a good idea, perhaps, at its inception, but after all this time why do we not change it?

It is a mindset that bicycle manufacturers seem unwilling to forfeit, despite the fact that most people who have used bicycles know that the seats are uncomfortable. The shape of a saddle suits the horse and rider and should not change . . . but the bicycle seat should.

There is a lot more to becoming a quality organisation than first meets the eye. It calls for an approach different from the 'warrant of fitness' type of quality systems so prevalent in modern companies, where the certificate on the wall often sets an expectation seldom met at the interface between employee and customer.

Quality is about disturbing the pattern of thinking, particularly at a management level, that it is a systems issue rather than a people issue. Fundamentally, quality is an issue of leadership.

❧ THE 'BOILED FROG' SYNDROME

THERE IS AN APOCRYPHAL STORY THAT IF YOU PLACE A FROG in a saucepan of water at room temperature, the frog will sit there reasonably contented.

If you place the saucepan, with the frog in the water, on a low heat, the frog will continue to sit in the warming water.

As the temperature is gradually increased, the frog's temperature-control mechanism adapts to meet the changing external temperature. So the water temperature rises and in response the frog's internal temperature adjusts, until the poor old frog ends up being boiled alive. (Do not try this at home.)

But if a frog is placed in a saucepan of boiling water, it will immediately jump out, hardly leaving time to be scalded.

The underlying theme of this tale is that you can be lulled into a false sense of comfort and complacency by adjusting unwittingly to small changes in your environment. Then suddenly, seemingly without warning, you are in Zone Two of the whirlpool and it is too late to affect your organisation's fate . . . to be sucked down the vortex of the whirlpool.

Quality programmes should not start with a systematic, procedural and policy review. That has a place . . . but not at the beginning. First is the need to ensure that management has a real concern for the customer. If they do not, then what example will be set for employees to follow? If management has a compelling and palpable concern for the customer, then this will inspire employees to share their concern.

The most important role a manager has in relation to quality is in attracting, hiring and retaining employees who share a true emotional commitment to quality and to exceptional service.

You can improve employee skills but I do not think you can easily teach them to like people. If they dislike people, how can they be exceptional service providers? I do not think they can.

❀ VACANCY: ONE LIGHTHOUSE OPERATOR

I WAS TALKING TO A GROUP OF PAYROLL MANAGERS ABOUT customer service. One of the managers obviously did not agree with my approach.

He said, 'Look, if someone telephones me and starts giving me a hard time about some error with their fortnightly pay, I just slam the phone down.'

He added, 'They will usually call back immediately and before they can start their complaint I tell them that unless they calm down, I will not speak to them . . . so they should take a minute to think about it, and then I click the phone off.'

I was deeply intrigued. The manager concluded by saying, ' . . . by the third call, they realise who is in charge and they identify their problem calmly and I deal with it as I get the opportunity.'

His extreme lack of concern for the customer was vaguely shocking. In this case it was an internal customer rather than an external one, but in my book the same rules apply.

I replied, 'It seems to me that if I were you I would never choose to work in payroll. The reason is that I do not think that I would like to deal with a litany of upset and angry people . . . because that is who you deal with in payroll.'

I continued, 'I cannot see you getting a call the day after pay-day that goes like this: "Morning, I expected my pay to be made yesterday. I have checked with my bank this morning and the correct amount has been deposited, exactly on the right date . . . I am calling to thank you very much for the excellent service . . . please have a very nice day."

'No. The people who call payroll are angry or upset or both because something has gone wrong with their pay.

'To work in payroll, one should have a very empathetic personality and a real desire to deal with angry and upset people in a sensitive but proficient manner.

'You, Sir,' I said, 'have the style and personality of someone who definitely should not work in payroll or any department that has a direct interface with internal or external customers . . . I suggest you apply to work in an isolated lighthouse on some remote uninhabited island!'

Quality comes down to leadership, leadership at all levels, believing and investing in people, rather than structures and systems; leaders who lead by example, whose behaviour aligns to the purpose and who realise that in any process, even processes that are in part or mostly automated, quality results are due to the people who plan, develop, implement, operate and maintain the process.

Quality planning must not be separated from the strategic, operational and performance planning process. It is as part of this process that quality becomes identified as a critical issue and is appropriately prioritised and resourced.

Standards of quality have been raised and will continue to be raised. As globalisation accelerates, survival without the highest quality standards will become increasingly difficult. No regional or national market can continue to be isolated against competitors from elsewhere, competitors who have a history and tradition of providing excep-tional service. *If they have not entered your market, they are about to.*

The public sector is not exempt from the requirements of quality.

The public sector is not exempt from the requirements of quality. This sector is still too strongly focused on the technical aspects of quality, rather than its delivery. This is what I have called the 'warrant of fitness' type of quality process which defines their capability to provide quality but makes no guarantee that delivery actually occurs.

Quality is not a focus on efficiency, structures, systems and procedures. Nor is it solely a focus on effectiveness, which fundamentally involves purpose and direction. It is a focus on the combination of efficiency and effectiveness, productivity.

Quality has been selected as the fifth line of leadership in The Whirlpool Effect™ model's cornerstone of Process. It is the line of leadership that requires the customer's perception to be considered as well as that of managers and employees.

Quality links strongly into the next, and last, line of leadership in The Whirlpool Effect™ model's cornerstone of Process . . . that is, *values.*

'What have values got to do with process?' I hear you say. 'Surely you mean policies? I can understand the role of purpose and planning, even process. But process needs policies to support the strategic and operational direction. Without policies,' I hear you say, 'there will be chaos.'

Policies are a major contributor to the bureaucracy of modern organisations. Employees and customers only really understand the content of policies when something goes wrong.

There is nothing wrong with guidance, but policies, once in place, create a rigidity that impedes risk-taking and experimentation — the cornerstones of innovation. I have never experienced policies creating a foundation for building a productive culture. This is because policies by their nature seek to achieve an accord on everything.

Policies create structural barriers and more often than not disempower frontline employees and also create significant and costly non-value-added activity. Management may seek a focus on the customer, but policies force a focus on the organisation or company. Too many policies diminish responsiveness and tend to extinguish the practice of 'common sense' by employees.

✿ A WINDOW, MY KINGDOM FOR A WINDOW

A COUPLE OF COLLEAGUES WHO WORKED TOGETHER TOLD ME this incredible story.

It was another forgettable Friday when Mike burst upon the scene and interrupted Steve, who was working in his small but well-organised workstation, fondly called the 'pen'. Mike worked in the adjacent 'pen', and had done so for the last two years.

Mike was excited, almost unable to contain himself. 'Guess what, you'll never guess, never . . . I have just heard that I have been promoted to manager, Product Research . . . but that's not it, I'm getting . . . wait for it . . . MY OWN OFFICE!'

Mike and Steve worked for a large multinational company which had very detailed and strict corporate policies. There was a serious hierarchy reflected in these policies, your position determining the size of your office, its location, the quality and quantity of furnishings . . . even down to a policy on the size and colour of the wastebasket.

Mike and Steve, as midline middle managers, were by policy decree entitled to a small workstation, basically an open workspace with panels but no walls. There was a built-in desk, a specified chair, filing cabinet and wastebasket. The workstations were all crammed into the centre of the floor with higher level middle managers' offices surrounding the 'pens'.

An office was a symbol of status and the first obvious 'badge' of a successful elevation in the hierarchy. 'Lifers' fantasised about the corner offices with the beautiful views from the windows on both walls . . . paradise . . . something to work for.

Mike said, 'This is not just an office, come and see . . . this is so good, it is unbelievable. I have to pinch myself to ensure I am not dreaming.'

Steve, excited for Mike, rushed off with Mike to see the office. When they reached the office, Steve was flabbergasted . . . totally blown away. Mike was entitled to an office for his new position and as it needed to be located in the Product Research building, he had been given the only available free space . . . the office next to the corner office, an office with a large window.

You are probably thinking, what is the big deal? Well, the big deal is that an office in this location and most of all an office with a window was, according to the corporate policy manual, the prize of a first-level senior executive, not an office 'first timer'.

But logic seemed to prevail. Mike needed to be in the

building, he was due to be given an office . . . so this was his lucky break.

Mike and Steve sat in the office until late in the evening, watching the view through the window as the sun set and darkness enveloped the scene. They drank several beers celebrating Mike's success and good luck.

Steve was working away the following Monday in his 'pen' when Mike arrived. He was pale and appeared to be in shock.

'Steve,' he mumbled, 'come and see my office.'

Steve followed Mike into his office and was shocked by what he saw. Over the weekend, the contractors had been in, under the instruction of senior management. They had put a false wall in place to reduce the size of the office to what Mike was allowed, according to the corporate policy manual. But worse, they had boarded over the window, which was a feature not available to someone of Mike's standing. They had also wallpapered the total office.

The previous furniture had been replaced by smaller and less specified furniture. The policy manual had been followed to the letter.

Steve shrugged his shoulders, comforted Mike and together they went to the cafeteria to buy a coffee and a newspaper. Almost in synchrony they opened the newspaper to the 'Situations Vacant' column.

The structural barriers erected by policies can frustrate and de-energise employees and impede the organisation's or company's potential to perform. Values are a much more effective tool than policies to align behaviour and develop consistency. Values, by their nature, have more elasticity than policies and thereby create synchrony without rigidity.

Policies make employees feel, and with justification, dependent. On the other hand, values, particularly shared values, make employees feel both independent and interdependent — and consequently, much more effective. If the underlying objective of policies is joint and consistent action, then substitute them with shared values and you will get a better deal.

Perhaps one of the most well known examples of the power of shared values is Ray Kroc, founder of the McDonald's fast-food chain. The key shared values of McDonald's are quality, service, value and cleanliness.

❀ I SEE A MESS, I CLEAN IT

THE STORY GOES THAT ONE DAY RAY KROC WALKED INTO ONE of his franchised stores during a busy period.

A thickshake had fallen off a table onto the floor, creating a real mess. This had gone unnoticed by the busy staff. Seeing the mess, Kroc went to the area where the cleaning implements were kept and cleaned the mess up himself.

When the staff realised that the man who had cleaned the mess was the founder and chairman of the total company, they would have been left in no doubt about the importance of cleanliness. Kroc's unspoken message was that cleanliness was so important that the chairman would clean the floor if necessary.

Values, to be meaningful, must be truly espoused by senior management, who must then always model the appropriate behaviour. Values create a sense of community where employees

Shared values create coordinates for frontline employees to make decisions without reference to unwieldly or unworkable policies

feel bound by factors other than job descriptions and policies. In this environment they will commit themselves to the objectives, goals and purpose of the company and do their best . . . more than that cannot be asked for.

The metaphor of community is more inspiring and meaningful than hierarchies and policies, more likely to unify a disparate group. Values are characterised as the 'way we behave around here'. They shape attitudes and behaviour and link to and support the purpose and planning process.

Shared values create coordinates for frontline employees to make decisions without reference to unwieldy or unworkable policies. They know what is important and by testing their options against the shared values are most likely to make the right decisions, most of the time.

Values create a forward momentum but do not eliminate diversity, for in most situations there is not a unitary solution. Shared values extinguish bureaucracy and support innovation; they are liberating to employees and highly supportive of quality and productivity.

Modern management has sensed the power of values, but still clings to the less relevant traditional management dogma, characterised by policies which create complex internal inter-dependencies. Values can minimise or eliminate these.

Values, like purpose, need to be shared and clear. Leaders have the ability to develop consensus on shared values and then to inspire employees to 'live the values'.

⚝ SLOGANS . . . SLOGANS . . . SLOGANS

One of the managers who worked with me at South Auckland Health unwittingly overheard the following conversation between a senior doctor and a junior.

Junior Doctor: 'This is a pretty good organisation, but it lacks a slogan that is pacy, descriptive and defines who we are.'

Senior Doctor: 'This is an organisation based on values, not slogans.'

Values are meaningful, important and themselves to be valued. Too often management lacks the energy and perseverance to engage in the long-term process of developing a shared understanding and commitment to its values. As is so often predictable in our 'instant society', they trivialise values by sloganeering to gain an early 'enhanced take-up'.

Values are not something that should be marketed or sold. They should simply be understood, and a long-term commitment made to them.

Slogans and values belong in different orbits.

While values are inherently logical and so 'win the mind', more importantly they are emotional and 'win the heart'. When the going gets tough, the latter is more important.

One of the advantages of values is that they allow for diversity within a range. However no employee or manager can be allowed to repeatedly breach the shared values. If they do, then clearly they do not share in the sense of community and common endeavour and there can be no place for them.

Values are not rules, they are simply a way of life. Create a climate where rules are made to be broken, but never values.

PART 5
PEOPLE

NINE | EMPOWERMENT IS NOT A CAPRICE

The people say, 'We did it ourselves.'

— Lao Tsu

Empowerment is a word often spoken by modern management, but it appears to be rarely meant. Is it merely overused as a management platitude, or is the word and — more importantly — the underlying concept, misunderstood?

It is not unreasonable to perceive that empowerment is just another passing fad of modern management, rather than a real opportunity to propel organisations or companies towards their destination, or even better, towards their true potential. Based on my experience, this is the area where the disconnection between management and employees is at its greatest.

All stakeholders can empirically understand the value in assisting employees, particularly those who interface directly with customers, to become more powerful. So where has this well-meaning management notion gone so wrong . . . is it the employees' fault? Have they failed when given the opportunity? I doubt this is the underlying problem. It is more likely that in most instances, empowerment has been misinterpreted by management as delegation. Delegation is a useful first step towards empowerment, but does not go far enough by any stretch of the imagination.

What then is empowerment? Simply, it is best defined as matching authority with responsibility . . . thereby achieving a matter of great importance in any organisation — clarifying notions of authority, accountability and responsibility. To be an exceptional service provider this type of clarity is not desirable, even essential . . . it is obligatory.

⟳ MY LIFE FOR A TELEPHONE

IN MY EARLY YEARS AS A MEDICAL STUDENT I WAS LIVING IN a flat. There was a waiting list for telephones and it seemed unlikely that I would get one in the short to medium-term future. I was living in South Africa at the time and telephone services were under the jurisdiction of the Post Office, an Oscar winner in every category of bureaucracy.

My brother, who had recently qualified as a dentist, was on his way to work in London. He suggested he would complete the request for a telephone in his name as he was a professional with a priority to receive a telephone, and could use it on his return. Great idea! We completed the necessary paperwork and some weeks later I received a letter advising me that my telephone would be installed in the next two weeks.

One day, on returning home, I saw that my telephone had indeed been installed. This was great stuff. I picked up the receiver and dialled the number of my friend to let him know I was now the proud owner of a telephone.

Oh no! There was no dialling tone. I checked the jack-point and the telephone itself, but everything appeared to be in order. I even unplugged the telephone and went across to a neighbour to check if the actual telephone worked . . . it did. I rang the Post Office, from the neighbour's, and explained the problem. They said they would check the job lot.

After a couple of minutes, the person on the other end of the phone — the consummate customer dissatisfier — told me that the request was clearly for a telephone installation and that had occurred.

I was bemused, but all became clear when she said, 'You have asked for a telephone to be installed, you have not asked for it to be connected.'

I was shocked. Who would want a telephone installed for ornamental value? This was bureaucracy at work and I despised it. Without any thought of the consequences I replied, 'My telephone is like your brain, installed but not connected.'

That unfortunate retort saw my telephone not connected for four and a half months, no matter what I did or who I wrote to, or called.

This unfortunate story illustrates how employees respond to oppressive and inflexible structures and systems. Who would possibly want a telephone installed, without it being connected? In this case the employee interpreted the instruction to install literally. With no further instruction on his job sheet to connect, he left having installed but not connected the telephone. The inability to use personal initiative and make common-sense decisions at 'the moment of truth' is merely a consequence of disempowerment over time.

The paradigm that promotes the view that managers do the thinking, supervisors the talking and employees the doing, creates the monster that provides the type of telephone installation service I received. Without authority being devolved to the employee along with responsibility, that responsibility will rest uncomfortably, and consequently unrealistically, on their shoulders. They will be left in a no-win situation. This is why there is often such a significant disconnection between management and employees on the issue of empowerment.

> **Management fears looking bad more than anything else.**

If management feels that they have empowered employees by passing them the responsibility, they are mistaken. The employees know that without the commensurate authority they will be unable or unlikely to deliver. In many ways, they are in a worse position and in fact have become truly disempowered.

If we reflect on my situation with the telephone installation, it does not require any great insight to realise that if, over time, those employees had the flexibility and latitude to meet customer needs, matched with the authority to serve their legitimate wants, then service responsiveness would have improved markedly.

Why does modern management continue to struggle with the concept of empowering their employees? It is a logical and understandable concept, grasped and appreciated by many. So why the difficulty in reality? Why is it that 'when the rubber hits the road', there is so little true empowerment?

My experience with modern management is they are primarily focused on micromanagement, peering ceaselessly down the microscope. This is what they know and feel comfortable doing. Why then pass this down the line . . . what will be left for the manager to do?

'If my employees do all of this, what will I do?' Interesting question.

Modern management has three basic fears, I think, in relation to employee empowerment — looking bad, looking bad and yes, looking bad. Management fears looking bad more than almost anything else. If the employee makes a mistake, particularly a big one, the manager looks bad. 'If my employee messes up . . . then I look bad.'

Even worse than the employee making a mistake is the employee doing a great job. Management fears this even more, because they have no one to blame. Furthermore, the better the job they do, the worse it makes the manager look. 'If my employee does a great job, then I look bad.'

Not quite as bad as the employee making a mistake, and certainly better than the employee doing a great job, the employee neither makes a mistake nor does a great job . . . but does not do it as well as the manager could. 'If my employee does not do as good a job as I could do, then I do not look good. If I do not look good, then I look bad.'

Underlying the fear of looking bad are two major reasons why modern management has such a strong desire to retain power . . . self-confidence (or more correctly, the lack of it), and the fear of losing.

Modern management has a desperate fear of losing. This is fundamental to why there is such a paucity of innovation. To innovate you must take risks and experiment, and you will experience losses . . . that is part of the territory. Until management can diminish its fear of losing, whatever that loss may manifest itself as . . . loss of face, loss of reputation, loss of customers, loss of profit . . . the need for power will never decrease.

The first and most important step for management to take in moving positively towards employee empowerment, is to eliminate the fear of losing. John Keats understood this when he said, 'Failure is, in a sense, the highway to success.'

The second step is for the manager to be self-confident. Self-confidence is the hallmark of the leader, and that self-confidence is based on trust. Trust in yourself and your capability, with a matching trust in your employees and their capabilities.

❧ I HAVE A RED FELT PEN, I AM EMPOWERED

SOME MONTHS AGO, I WAS VISITING ANOTHER CITY ON business. I concluded my business rather earlier than expected, so headed off to the airport to return home.

My airline ticket reservation was for a return flight at 6.00 pm.

On reaching the airport, I went to the ticketing department to see if I could possibly arrange an earlier flight. I approached the counter and was greeted by a friendly service assistant. I explained my situation and after a quick look at her wristwatch, she expertly tapped at the computer keyboard.

She told me that there was only one other airplane returning to my home city before 6.00 pm, and that it was due to depart at 3.30 pm, which was in slightly less than ten minutes. She explained that a seat was available and although the boarding call had already been made, I could make the flight.

In order to be able to check in, I needed to first be re-ticketed, which she would do. As my reservation was made on a special deal, any change would require a further charge of forty-five dollars. I confirmed that I was happy to pay the extra.

While she tapped on her keyboard, I got my wallet from my jacket pocket and took out my credit card, to ensure I wasted no time. I was now mentally committed to the 3.30 pm flight . . . two and a half hours saved . . . great!

She seemed to be having a problem with her computer, time was marching on and I was now becoming anxious. I prompted her with my concerns.

'There's now only five minutes until the flight takes off, I need the ticket, I need time to pay, to get to the check-in counter, to check in and then to get to the departure gate and embark onto the plane. Will I have enough time?' I asked.

Without hesitation, she grabbed a red felt-tip pen and wrote across my existing ticket . . . FLIGHT 457 . . . in large lettering.

'Sir, take this directly to the plane, do not go to the check-in counter, go directly to the plane. This will serve as your new ticket as well as your boarding card. I will call the plane to advise them of this, and also that you are to be expected.'

'What about the extra forty-five dollars?' I asked.

She replied, 'That has just been waived.'

I was naturally grateful and thanked her profusely. Before leaving for the plane I asked whether she had been having problems with her computer. She replied that she had; for some reason it would not accept the requested change, no matter what she did.

I asked her what authority she had to break a number of rules. Not issuing a valid ticket, overriding the check-in process and waiving the fee. I asked her this because at no time did she consult any supervisor or manager.

She replied that she had full authority, responsibility

> and accountability for customer service, and if what it took
> to get me on the plane was a litany of rule-breaking, then
> she had the authority to do that.

A real-life, stunning example of a truly empowered employee! Liberated, free as a bird . . . an employee with the capacity to act like an owner, to do what was best for the business.

If she had said to me that because the computer was unwilling to cooperate I was unable to catch the early flight, I would have been a dissatisfied customer. It was not her that had failed, it was the system. But the flawed system, which underlies so many issues that result in poor customer service, does not have to be where the matter ends, as this story shows.

Obviously the airline employee had been unshackled and liberated from an overbearing, non-responsive structure and was free to act in the interests of the customer. Some of you might say, but hey, she lost a sale. I would say to you that that is irrelevant, because she won a happy customer. From a sale, comes one sale . . . from a happy customer, comes a stream of sales. If I had a choice, I know which I would choose.

What modern management needs to contemplate is that if you truly empower your employees, it confirms their underlying worth. This will inspire them, and by developing a climate of trust, build their self-confidence. They will then have pride in what they do — and never, never underestimate the power of people with pride . . . pride is the most stable platform for the development of peak performance, which is essential for exceptional, world-class performance in any organisation or company.

The relationship between modern management and employees has focused too strongly on developing *competence*, and has placed insufficient emphasis on the development of *self-confidence*. Competence and confidence together are a powerful cocktail.

> **What modern management needs to contemplate is that if you truly empower your employees, it confirms their underlying worth.**

Empowerment, not delegation, is the first line of leadership in The Whirlpool Effect™ model's cornerstone of People. The fascinating thing about empowerment is that you do not necessarily have to pass power to employees . . . they already have it. The problem is they do not realise it. Even if they did, there is sometimes not much they can do about it because the structures and systems modern management has set in place are actually impediments to employees getting on with providing exceptional customer service.

Management needs simply to free up employees to exercise the power they already have. Enlightened management, as illustrated in the re-ticketing story, know how simple it really is. But first, management must itself be self-confident and must have no fear of losing. Leaders have no problem with empowerment if they are self-confident themselves.

The large rump of modern management is scared of risk. The concern about losing is so large that there appears to be little time spent or focus on winning. To empower others is to take a risk. For empowerment to work on a sustainable basis, management must accept any failures or mistakes as a consequence of empowerment without resorting to punishing those who have failed or erred . . . empowerment will not work in a climate of fear.

Empowerment is like teamwork, it requires practice. With practice people can get rather good at it. Managers must apply common sense and encourage their employees' judgment. They must look behind the fixed cost of employee Number 124, Grade III clerk, and see the human being with a mind, a heart and a soul . . . someone with capacity to be a peak performer, given the right environment.

What is the right environment, you may ask. It is one of trust. Trust means not seeing employees as heads and hands but as hearts and souls. Trust is an emotional bond and relates very much to consistency and predictability.

That is why in times of change, the trust that exists can be placed under threat. This threat can be managed by being open and honest and by ensuring that when employees are told something will happen, it does. Trust is inextricably linked to honesty and responsibility, with integrity being at the core of its long-term development.

❧ YES, YOU CAN WIELD A SCALPEL, BUT NOT A TELEPHONE

WHEN I WORKED AS CHIEF EXECUTIVE OF SOUTH AUCKLAND Health, one of my first experiences was trying to make a long-distance telephone call.

I could not get through and eventually gave up in frustration. On checking, I found out that the telephone had a toll bar, to prevent individual employees making toll calls.

To make a toll call, I found out you had to call the operator, identify yourself, provide the number you required to be called and they would then place the call . . . directly, or when they had the opportunity, in which case they would call you back.

What a bureaucratic system, time-consuming and inefficient for all concerned!

The telephone operators spent so much time dealing with internal call requests that incoming calls were being answered far too slowly.

Putting all that aside, the underlying rationale here was less than compelling. You are a highly qualified surgeon, trusted to undertake complex invasive surgery, trusted to save patient's lives . . . but not trusted to make a toll call. Someone in management obviously thought that the doctors, the major users of toll calls, would abuse the system and make personal calls!

I cannot see how you can develop trust in an environment where there are explicit signals that you do not have integrity. Anyhow, to my mind, if the surgeon needs to call her father in another city to check that he is recovering from his recent illness, then why shouldn't she? She will be more relaxed in the operating theatre, having resolved her personal concerns.

Doctors need toll-free access to call other doctors long-distance regarding patient care, patient transfer, seeking and offering clinical advice . . . why erect an unnecessary barrier? The only reason is because management felt that they could not trust the doctors to not abuse the system.

Toll bars were removed. What were the consequences?

- the climate of trust improved
- doctors became more efficient
- the telephone system for incoming calls improved
- the toll bill did not increase

Funny that . . . modern management talks about motivating employees but they need to have as their primary concern to stop demotivating them.

> **By management developing trust and liberating employees from excessive control, an environment will develop where employees go well beyond the 'call of duty'.**

Actually, research has shown that companies that allowed higher spending authorities for employees outperformed those that did not.

Trust and empowerment are linked . . . and *trust* is the second line of leadership in The Whirlpool Effect™ model's cornerstone of People. By management developing trust and liberating employees from excessive control, an environment will develop where employees go well beyond the 'call of duty'. That is where employees need to be for an organisation or company to reach its potential.

You may ask why it has taken almost nine chapters before I turn on employees instead of managers . . . a welcome change, some might say. It is because I believe that modern management is primarily responsible for the failure of organisations and companies to deliver to their potential . . . not employees.

Employees, however, do have a number of elements within their domain of influence, and one of them is to recognise that the well-being of management is to the advantage of employees, on the same basis that the well-being of employees is to the advantage of management. The attitude of some employees and unions to forming the trust relationship is less than helpful. Frankly, it is entirely self-defeating.

It is also worth a reminder that if there is no sense of common purpose, there could be chaos, if true empowerment was set in place. Employees who are not aligned and are empowered, are likely to be as destructive as bureaucracy itself.

All parties need to face up to the trust issue . . . it is a shared responsibility. When trust starts to develop in an organisation or company it can become a potent contagion, spreading from one part of the organisation to another.

Trust can have a powerful relaxing effect on organisations, improving communication, stimulating creativity and innovation, encouraging teamwork, courtesy and genuine concern for others . . . especially customers.

Employees, however, do have a number of elements within their domain of influence, and one of them is to recognise that the well-being of management is to the advantage of employees, on the same basis that the well-being of employees is to the advantage of management.

The third line of leadership in The Whirlpool Effect™ model's cornerstone of People is *dignity*. The effective leader does not rely on their position for authority; they tend, rather, to rely on fostering and nurturing relationships with employees of all levels of ability and responsibility . . . not only with their directly reporting line managers. These relationships are based on trust and communication, allowing relationships to develop on a basis of equality rather than hierarchy. This type of relationship creates a deep sense of dignity for employees, which itself is a compelling force that drives commitment.

Leaders care deeply and are sensitive to the individual dignity of employees and the collective dignity of teams. They are aware that employees at all levels have something meaningful to contribute, and they encourage this actively, not as a matter of process, but rather as a matter of respect.

TEN

WELL-POISONERS, LAWNMOWERS AND LANDSCAPERS

An army marches as fast as its slowest soldier.

— Anonymous

Sadly, many modern managers, influenced by poorly thought through, unvalidated business theory, have a view that the hierarchy of importance in respect of their organisation or company is:

- shareholders
- customers
- employees or . . .

- shareholders
- competitors
- customers or . . .

- competitors
- shareholders
- customers or . . .

- customers
- shareholders
- employees

My own view is that the hierarchy should look more like this:

- organisation/company
- employees
- customers
- shareholders

Far too many managers regard their organisation or company as inert, rather than a live organism in its own right. Perhaps it is because of an unwitting, deadly weakness of paying little attention to anything other than tangible results and perform-ance. An unceasing focus on the analytical and the rational encourages a very myopic view of what an organisation or company actually is.

It is not, in my mind, an orderly construct of balance sheets and operating statements, of bricks and mortar, heads and hands, equipment and information.

No, no, no . . . an organisation or company is alive, it is a life in itself. It is definitely not inert. It is conceived from a dream, nursed with a plan; it grows up supported by values. It has a history and tradition, it has pride and meaning ... like all living organisms, it requires love, attention and care. It can be in full robust health, it can become ill or disabled and may even die.

As a manager of an organisation you are responsible for a living organism . . . a life. This is a responsibility worth having. Think about an organisation or company as inert, lifeless or think of it as alive, a life. The difference is a leap of logic, and one seldom made.

Most parents who have a new baby want to protect it, to ensure its health. What do they do? They immunise their baby against killer diseases like polio, diphtheria, tetanus, smallpox. They do not want these potentially deadly, but preventable, environmental threats to harm their precious baby, to weaken, disable or kill it. It is no different with an organisation or company. If you view it as alive, a living organism, your interest will lie in protecting it against potentially deadly environmental threats.

Modern management can identify with this. Certainly they are very comfortable with the concept of environmental threats in the form of competitors. But paranoia about competitors is rather misplaced. If, as a manager, your peripheral vision is totally obscured by competitors and if that is the point of commencement of your thinking, then more often than not you will be in a reactive rather than proactive position.

> A purpose of the deepest clarity, compellingly inspirational and inarguably credible, linked to an imaginative plan, immersed in the wisdom of Solomon, meticulous in its detail, tied to process so elegantly, coordinated and steeped in values . . . can be destroyed like a house of cards by letting the wrong people into an organisation.

If on the other hand you start by thinking of your own organisation or company and how you can assist it to remain healthy and to grow to be strong, then more often than not you will find yourself in a proactive role.

The most important decision a manager makes is about who she lets into the organisation or company. Yes, recruitment is the most important single decision — and one so often delegated to a third party, internal or external. I find this so incredibly perplexing. A purpose of the deepest clarity, compellingly inspirational and inarguably credible, linked to an imaginative plan, immersed in the wisdom of Solomon, meticulous in its detail, tied to process so elegantly, coordinated and steeped in values . . . can be destroyed like a house of cards by letting the wrong people into an organisation. Like a newborn baby, an organisation or company, alive and vulnerable, must be immunised against potential deadly environmental threats — the wrong people. This obligatory vaccination is termed *preventative recruitment* and is the fourth line of leadership of The Whirlpool Effect™ model's fourth and final cornerstone, *People*.

Preventative recruitment is simply keeping the wrong people out. Let them in and they will rapidly infect the organisation or company with their negativity, pessimism, scepticism and 'can't do' attitude. They will insidiously weaken the company and can ultimately bring it to its knees.

WELL-POISONERS, LAWNMOWERS, LANDSCAPERS

There are people in organisations and companies, in communities and in countries, who place poison in the wells from which all of us collect our drinking water. Their objective is fundamental — they want to make us ill, they wish to weaken and disable us, and they may even have as an objective to end our life.

These people are called 'well-poisoners'. They are bad people who are consumed by self-interest and negativity; they are destructive and sadly they have no remorse. They are the corporate sociopaths and psychopaths and there is no room for them.

They are resistant to inspiration, sharing and teamwork but strangely, they are seldom stupid or lacking in talent. Unfortunately their intellect and talent are channelled into power and empire-building. They are pathologically territorial.

Well-poisoners are insanely competitive — about things that do not matter. They are perpetually angry and on attack. They always put themselves and their cause first. They are back-stabbers, exploitative and manipulative. There is no place for this type of employee. Keep them out of your organisation or company and if they are already within it, ensure their release. They are unmanageable, because they are treacherous.

Fortunately, the number of true well-poisoners in any organisation or company is small, but the negative impact they have is inversely proportionate to their number.

The next group to be found in organisations and companies, in communities and countries are called 'lawnmowers'. Think about lawnmowing for a moment. Most people who mow their lawns regularly develop a repeatable pattern. They start at one end, mow up and down in straight rows and then finish at the other end. Week after week or fortnight after fortnight, the same pattern is repeated.

I know this, for I have watched large numbers of people mowing their lawns. Take time off and watch your neighbours mow the lawn. Almost invariably, there is the same pattern, start . . . up and down . . . finish. How often do you see people mowing their lawns in triangular patterns, in wild spirals like spaghetti, in figures-of-eight? Seldom, if ever.

Yes, most people are 'maintainers' or 'lawnmowers'. These are good people, capable, willing to coordinate and be a member of the team, able to share and align themselves to the purpose. They are assiduous about reflecting the shared values. They have their different perspectives and views which they articulate constructively.

Lawnmowers form the majority of most organisations and companies, they are good, very good people . . . they are the followers.

I admire and salute the lawnmowers. In my experience, they have high standards and a capacity for work. They are the mind and muscle of most organisations. Because they are generally positive and cooperative, they do not attract the same management attention as well-poisoners . . . this is a shame, because they are the people who deserve the attention.

I love these people with a passion, but I despise well-poisoners whom I hold in absolute contempt.

The third group in any organisation or company, community or country are the 'landscapers'.

This group can take a desolate piece of land and with their

149

creativity, judgment, courage, brilliance and hard work — supported by the lawnmowers — are able to transform it into a beautiful, flourishing, sustainable and productive garden.

Landscapers are the rarest of the three groups; they are the leaders.

While well-poisoners cannot evolve into lawnmowers, some lawnmowers can evolve into landscapers.

> **I do not believe the hiring decision can or should be delegated.**

I do not believe the hiring decision can or should be delegated. Certainly seek advice, but retain, at all costs, the hiring decisions within the line function. Human resource departments are staff rather than line functions. I do not believe that they can ever make as relevant a hiring decision as the line manager. Certainly it may be appropriate to delegate elements of the recruitment process to the human resource department. But beware of them hijacking the process — this happens all too frequently. Get involved and stay involved in the recruitment process, ensuring that recruitment decisions end up solving more problems than they cause.

In practice, far too many managers are focused on the short term and consequently often see the recruitment process as filling a vacancy. They place too much emphasis on technical capability — the ability to do the job — rather than on the attitude of wanting to be part of the organisation or company.

In my experience, it is easier to match ability than attitude. Ability is how you do things, while attitude is the way you think about things, how you act and react.

❦ I SEE A PROBLEM . . . I AM A PROBLEM IDENTIFIER

A young manager is invited by his boss for a drive in his brand-new Volvo station wagon. He is looking forward to this as he has been promised the opportunity to take the wheel of this brand new car. Being a young man he has never driven a new car before, let alone a Volvo.

They are accompanied on the drive by his boss's wife, who sits in the rear passenger seat.

The young manager is really enjoying the drive, except for the fact that the boss's wife is constantly moaning about the garbage littering the footpath, as a result of the now ten-day-old garbage collectors' strike. She is complaining of the smell, the mess, the danger of disease. Eventually the young manager cannot stand another minute of this.

He slams on the brake, opens his door and jumps out of the car, rushing to the back of the station wagon to open the tailgate. He then goes over to the sidewalk and lifts up an armful of the rotting garbage. He goes back to the station wagon and throws the armful of garbage into the back.

He manages to repeat this before being accosted by the now angry wife and shocked boss.

'What in heaven's name are you doing?' demands the wife.

'Well, you have identified the rotting garbage as a significant problem,' says the young manager, 'and I have identified a solution.

'We have the station wagon, time and my labour . . . I am prepared to collect the garbage and drop it off at the refuse tip. I will do as many trips as I can today and on

Sunday . . . that should clear the mess, at least in this part of your suburb.'

'No way,' says the wife.

'What do you mean, no way?' asks the young manager. 'Do you not want me to do this?'

'Absolutely right,' says the wife. 'I want you to take us home, clean this car, bring it back to its new condition . . . and then I never want to see you again.'

'Let me understand,' says the young manager. 'You do not wish me to implement my solution . . . in other words you do not really care enough about the problem to want to solve it?'

'Yes, take me home,' says the wife.

Many individuals in organisations are like the boss's wife in this story. They do not have the right attitude — they love to complain and they relish identifying problems. However, when it comes to the solution, they generally find that the effort and consequences of putting in place a solution are often unpalatable to them.

Attitude is what makes the difference . . . the right attitude.

A great attitude is the prescription for success, while great ability may not translate into a positive outcome if complemented by a bad attitude.

A potential employee with ability, but whose attitude will not reinforce the common purpose and most importantly the shared values of the company, should be overlooked. The best organisations and companies recruit to fit the organisation or company, rather than just the job.

Recruitment is the most difficult part of the role of a

manager and the most important. Place an emphasis on honesty, dependability, cooperativeness and competence. These are important qualities for teamwork, the foundation of success in almost every organisation.

Self-confidence is a very important quality, and it is a different quality from competence. Self-confidence relates to the belief a person has in their abilities.

The single most important quality I seek in potential employees at any level, however, is self-awareness. People who are not clearly aware of how they are perceived and who are not clear about their own strengths and weaknesses, become high-maintenance employees and are unlikely to deliver to their potential. The reason is that they often do not have the right attitude.

Never, never, recruit in isolation. You must involve others and create a forum for getting it right. Make the firing decision when you make the hiring decision.

Preventative recruitment means keeping the wrong people out of your organisation or company. If you have the slightest doubt about an individual, do not hire them. Trust your judgment and back yourself and never allow anyone to talk you into a recruit you have even the slightest discomfort with.

Attracting the right employee is a tough enough job, but it does not end there. Next, you face another tough assignment — retaining them. The better they are, the more difficult this can be, mainly because of the frequent approaches that they will receive from other organisations.

The fifth line of leadership in The Whirlpool Effect™ model's cornerstone of People is *employee retention*. Remember, the organisation is alive and like all living organisms requires care and attention to keep it that way. Like the human body, an organisation or company requires the correct nourishment to remain healthy.

A management style and an organisational or company culture developed to retain employees is a distinct competitive advantage.

In the human body, nutrition aims to deliver essential carbohydrates, proteins, fats, vitamins and minerals to the basic building block of the human body, the cell. In an organisation or company the basic building block is the individual employee, and they too require essential elements to keep them, and as a consequence, the organisation, in good health. The individual employee needs these elements not to stay alive, because they have the capacity to do that in another organisation or company, but to be retained.

Modern management is well aware of the costs of employee turnover, especially when replacing lost employees. However, they seem to lose interest in the underlying issue as soon as the vacancy is filled. The costs of employee turnover, both tangible and intangible (often the most costly), are an issue of strategic importance to management.

A management style and an organisational or company culture developed to retain employees is a distinct competitive advantage. Employees understand this, but too few modern managers do. Management seems convinced that the only way to engender loyalty amongst employees is through contractual relationships or, more commonly, through extrinsic rewards. Extrinsic rewards, in particular pay, are important, but they are only part of an overall picture. Money does shape behaviour and impacts on self-worth, but then so do intrinsic rewards.

It is important to get the structure of pay right and to ensure it is aligned to the purpose, goals, objectives and values of the organisation or company. My advice in relation to pay is to keep it simple. Many performance-related pay systems reach such levels of complexity that they are a negative rather than a positive factor.

> Many performance-related pay systems reach such levels of complexity that they are a negative rather than a positive factor.

Never, never, create a performance-related pay system in an environment where responsibility and accountability are not matched with authority. This is a lose-lose situation and a quick way to disaffect good, effective people.

Yes, it is important to pay effective people appropriately and it is something that is necessary to retaining employees, but its importance is often misunderstood and overrated. This is because it is only one element, albeit a very important one. Imagine a cell in the human body that depends on a mix of essential elements to keep it alive. Provide that cell with more protein than it requires and no other nutrients and it will die.

Employees are similar to the cell: to retain them they need the right pay, but that is not all they need. They need dignity and respect; they need to be trusted and to be believed in; they need to be informed; they need to be understood and most of all . . . they need to be appreciated. Employees need a way of life that supports them, their goals and ambitions, and those of their families. They also need your support — they need you to back them, not blame them. They require help and protection, particularly those who have a high level of customer contact.

Coal-face employees can become exhausted from the day-to-day stress, especially those employees who deal frequently with customers who have problems and complaints or are annoyed for whatever reason.

155

🌀 MY BAGS ARE PACKED, I'M READY TO GO

A FRIEND OF MINE WAS STANDING IN LINE TO CHECK IN FOR an overseas flight at the airport. The man in front of her was in a foul temper and was both rude and aggressive to the check-in assistant.

When my friend reached the counter to check in herself, she asked the assistant if he received that sort of treatment often. He indicated that he did receive that kind of attack reasonably frequently, but added that he was used to it . . . and in any event it was company policy that the customer was always right, irrespective of the situation.

My friend indicated that she did not think that had been the case with the previous customer, sensing that the assistant, in his heart of hearts, really thought the same.

The assistant assured my friend that she should not be concerned about him, adding that he was well able to handle himself and in any event, he said, 'I have destressed myself already. He is travelling to London and his luggage is travelling to Tokyo.'

It is in the crucial frontline positions, on which organisations and companies are so dependent, that retention is most difficult. In these areas intrinsic elements of the job are incredibly powerful in retaining employees — elements such as rotating employees who have high-level customer contact jobs into less stressful positions for a period. Providing more than the usual number of interesting breaks, and holidays to be taken at more frequent intervals than usual. Offering exceptional training and development — provided this is matched with opportunity.

Feedback — positive feedback — is an intrinsic element for

all employees at all levels of ability and responsibility. Feedback must, as frequently as possible, be immediate. When you place your coins in a vending machine, you expect the choice you have made to drop into the pick-up bay immediately. Feedback, to be effective, should not be delayed until the performance appraisal . . . it needs to be immediate, personal and sincere.

Extrinsic rewards can be extremely divisive if handled inappropriately. Everyone in an organisation knows what is going on, but managers seem surprised to find out that 'confidential' deals with certain individuals become widely known. The best way of overcoming this is to reward the complete team, not only the star. Realistically, in most organisations or companies the success of an individual is almost always the result of the contribution of many others who are 'behind the scenes'.

An important intrinsic element is giving employees the opportunity to participate and contribute. This is incredibly important to employees but it must be a real rather than a token opportunity, otherwise it becomes another powerful reason for them to take their skills and qualities elsewhere.

Perhaps the task modern management finds most difficult to confront is releasing employees who have failed in their job. It is unusual for employees to fail as a result of deficient technical skills; they generally fail because their attitude fails to fit with the value system and style of the organisation. It is understandable that management hesitates to fire those who fail to perform in their jobs. But remember, an organisation or company is alive, a living organism, and management has a responsibility to keep it alive and healthy.

But if the human body develops a localised infection, it can become an abscess. The abscess will start with symptoms of irritation, building to pain and swelling. If the appropriate early intervention is not taken, the abscess will reach a point where its toxins enter the bloodstream. The localised infection is now a systemic problem causing ill-health to the whole body. The person with an advanced abscess can become quite unwell.

At this point, anti-infective medications will not be able to manage this advanced problem. Immediate action is required. A surgeon will incise the abscess with a scalpel, releasing the infected contents. With the source of the toxins removed, the body will rapidly improve and soon return to good health.

An organisation or company is no different to the human body. If there is an employee who is a 'well-poisoner', they too release toxins into the wider organisation or company, causing generalised ill-health. These 'well-poisoners' must be released, not transferred (or even worse, promoted). Modern management thinks it can throw new blankets over 'old horses', but this only serves to exacerbate, rather than solve, the real problem.

If an employee is to be released, it must be handled in a candid, compassionate and transparent manner . . . but it must be done quickly. 'Well-poisoners' capture the attention and time of management, they demotivate their co-workers and they prevent an organisation or company from reaching its potential. *Releasing* them is the sixth line of leadership in The Whirlpool Effect™ model's cornerstone of People.

PART 6
LEADERSHIP

ELEVEN | SHAPED TO LEAD, SUITED TO FOLLOW

Leaders have much more in common with artists,
scientists, and other creative thinkers than they do with
managers.

— Abraham Zaleznik

This is an enduring debate . . . is there a difference between
leaders and managers. Are leaders born, or can leadership be
learned?

According to Field Marshal Lord Slim, 'There is a difference
between leadership and management. The leader and those who
follow represent one of the oldest, most natural, and most
effective human relationships. The manager and those managed
are a later product with neither so romantic or inspiring a
history. Leadership is of the spirit, compounded of personality
and vision — its practice is an art. Management is of the mind,
more a matter of accurate calculation, statistics, methods,
timetables and routine — its practice is a science.'

For most of us, the word 'leader' tends to evoke an image of
someone who is inspiring, visionary, courageous, creative and

161

optimistic . . . someone worth following. The word 'manager' on the other hand suggests a quite different image . . . steady, rational, analytical, ordered, inflexible and controlling . . . someone you follow because you have to.

I personally feel certain that there is a significant difference between leadership and management and also that it is leadership, not management, that will provide the platform for an organisation or company to reach its potential.

You might ask then, what are the fundamental qualities of a leader, and more importantly, can these, through learning and experience, become skills that can be mastered?

> **My own view is that there are people who, for a number of reasons, are shaped to lead, just as other people are more suited to follow.**

My own view is that there are people who, for a number of reasons, are shaped to lead, just as other people are more suited to follow. But those people who have the inherited or naturally acquired qualities of leadership are not automatically leaders. To be a leader requires an individual to make a voluntary decision to lead. Being placed in a position of responsibility, for example being appointed chief executive, does not mean you are a leader, even if you have the required attributes and qualities . . . all it means is that you have a high-level appointment. It means you have authority . . . but it does not necessarily mean you have credibility.

❧ YOUR COUNTRY NEEDS YOU!

MY FRIEND WAS SERVING IN THE MILITARY AND HAD recently completed his basic training. Prior to being posted, he had been assigned to guard duty.

It was a little after midnight, on a winter's night, and he was guarding a seldom-used side gate entry to the camp.

He had been on the duty for weeks, night after night, guarding the entrance. In the time that he had been there, the gate had not been used at all.

He was cold and bored as he stood there, no longer expecting anything other than becoming colder and more bored . . . when a large black limousine pulled up to the gate. My friend walked to the driver's side. The window was lowered to reveal a military chauffeur. My friend asked him for his identification and permission to enter. The driver courteously provided these.

Noticing someone sitting in the back seat, my friend stepped to one side and knocked on the back seat window. The window was lowered to reveal a man in full military dress. My friend became nervous when he saw this man's epaulettes, which were crowded with gold stars and braid He was so highly ranked, my friend could not immediately even identify what his rank was.

With a quiver in his voice, my friend asked the high-ranking officer for his identification and his permission to enter. Without even turning his face towards my friend, he tapped three times on his left epaulette with his right index finger, implying that he did not need identification or proof of permission to enter.

My friend, now more confident, asked him again to provide identification and permission to enter. The officer looked straight ahead and rudely thumped his left epaulette with his right hand.

My friend patiently explained that he was under the strictest orders not to allow entry to anyone without the appropriate documentation being sighted. There could be no exceptions, even high-ranking officers. He again requested the officer to provide the documentation, to prove he was not an imposter.

The officer, now visibly angry, again thumped his epaulette.

My friend at this point walked to the front of the limousine, fixing his bayonet to his rifle. He then without warning charged at the stationary vehicle, forcefully stabbing the bayonet through the grille into the radiator. After a flurry of thrusts, water drained out of the radiator, leaving the car paralysed.

My friend had this vision of receiving a ten-day leave pass for his strict application of duty and clear following of instruction. This man could be a terrorist, my friend could have saved the military camp from an act of sabotage . . . what a hero. Perhaps a medal, as well as a leave pass?

The next day he was summoned by the military commander of the camp, who immediately sentenced him to ten days in detention barracks.

There is an important differentiation between a person's power of rank and the credibility of a leader. The former wields authority and the subordinates comply, the latter applies influence and his subordinates commit to a cause — a big difference.

To become the leader, you need to make a decision to lead.

If your employees make a voluntary decision to follow you, then, and only then, has leadership occurred. Making a decision to exercise your authority and forcing employees to act on instruction is not leadership.

Making a decision to exercise your authority and forcing employees to act on instruction is not leadership.

Personal experience, observation and careful thought and reflection have led me to determine that the fundamental qualities of a leader are:

- integrity
- vision
- courage
- the ability to inspire others
- a strong sense of individuality
- self-awareness
- self-confidence
- the ability to listen with a 'third' ear
- optimism
- passion
- instinct
- an exceptional sense of judgment
- an impeccable sense of timing
- a deep sense of service
- intelligence
- perseverance
- thoughtfulness
- self-control
- caring
- humility
- respect
- unselfishness

- loyalty
- resilience
- decisiveness
- a daring sense of adventure
- humour
- tact
- fairness
- ability to process and retain information
- focus
- preparedness to accept full and final responsibility
- consistency
- calmness
- pro-activity
- patience
- willingness to trust
- flexibility
- balance
- willingness to learn

This frightening list of forty qualities of leadership reinforces the challenge of being a true leader.

What is even more daunting is to understand that of these forty qualities, there are ten that I believe are not able to be easily mastered through learning and experience. It is my belief that these are inherited or 'naturally' acquired, much like a talent for sport, music or art.

There are people by virtue of their inherited attributes who have exceptional eye-hand-foot coordination. They have a natural gift for ball sports, or for one ball sport in particular. With practice and interest they can achieve their potential. However, someone lacking the natural skills, despite practice and commitment, is unlikely to reach the same level of performance. They could become competent, but are most unlikely to reach the top. We accept and understand that.

There are people who have inherited musical qualities, or the ability to paint or sculpt. Tuition and practice will lead to improvement, but if the natural talent is not there, do not expect them to challenge the best. Basic natural ability is required — we accept and understand that. He is not musical, she is not artistic, he lacks the necessary eye-hand-ball coordination, she is not agile enough . . . these are not insults, they are merely a reflection of reality.

As with all sweeping generalisations, there will be exceptions and we understand that too.

Managers with these natural talents or gifts will generally outperform those managers who do not have them. But we continue to delude ourselves, and rob our organisations and companies of an opportunity to reach their potential, by not recognising and accepting this.

No one would place tone-deaf individuals in a philharmonic orchestra, nor would they ask someone who lacked both coordination and agility to perform gymnastics on the parallel bars. If someone lacked physical endurance, asking them to run a marathon would not make sense, particularly if they were aiming to be world class, an exceptional performer, a winner.

Those managers who do not have the following natural qualities, I believe, are less likely to become successful leaders than those that do:

- intelligence
- integrity
- vision
- courage
- the ability to inspire others
- optimism
- self-awareness
- the ability to listen with a 'third' ear

- instinct
- an exceptional sense of judgment

These ten qualities are the most difficult to acquire by learning or through experience. Why do organisations therefore not specifically attract employees with these qualities, nurture them and then liberate them into leadership positions, allowing the organisation to be propelled towards its potential?

The reason is simple. Most organisations or companies find employees with these gifts of leadership difficult to manage. These people are often characterised as 'mavericks' and management puts significant effort into trying to control and constrain them.

This is wrong. Such individuals symbolise innovation, they are the leaders of the future, they need to learn and gain experience . . . they should be fostered wherever they occur. By their nature, they are unorthodox. They are bold and daring and their willingness to experiment and take risks is often viewed with alarm and concern. They frighten the traditional manager with their vision and ability to inspire, through which they often become a focus for referred power.

Sadly, and all too frequently, those employees with that uncommon blend of the ten key qualities of leadership, the 'inner circle qualities of leadership', leave organisations or companies for no other reason than senior management, despite what they say, fearing the consequences of nurturing and promoting these individuals with that rare ability to stretch their thinking beyond that which is known today.

They strike fear into the hearts and souls of modern management by being obsessed with finding the right questions, rather than the right answers. Their driving curiosity and experimentation can perplex and frustrate management, who respond by placing bureaucratic barriers or hurdles in their path. Their boundless energy, comfort with ambiguity and their action-orientated, results-driven approach may even cause envy amongst those senior managers who, when you lift the veil, are often motivated by self-interest and their own personal career, and find the 'competition' discomforting.

Such individuals are most often artful, empathetic and inspiring communicators, exceptional listeners with the rare ability to connect one on one with employees at all levels of ability and responsibility. They are often complex people able to achieve high levels of personal credibility.

At the very core of leadership is the drive to *shape* rather than to *control*, the desire to create interdependencies rather than dependencies, the wish to restructure how people frame their thoughts, rather than restructure organisations.

Modern management must learn not to fear these individuals, not to be concerned that they are 'difficult to manage' . . . they must foster them, if they wish to retain them. They do not respond well to being bureaucratically imprisoned, much like a lion captured from the wild and caged in a zoo. When that lion loses its freedom, it no longer experiences what it is like to be a lion and stops acting like a lion in the wild. It is no different with potential leaders. If they are constrained and limited they will not experience the privilege of being a leader and that potential can be extinguished or lost to another organisation or company . . . usually their own, and then you have real competition.

The 'inner circle qualities', those I believe are inherited or naturally acquired, by themselves will not create a leader. Those thirty learned qualities are also necessary to shape an effective leader.

I think that the whole concept of leadership is still misunderstood, largely obscured by an orthodox and traditional view of what management is. At the very core of leadership is the drive to *shape* rather than to *control*, the desire to create inter-dependencies rather than dependencies, the wish to restructure how people frame their thoughts, rather than restructure organisations. Leadership in this sense is more subtle than most modern management allows and more complex. It is more flexible too, unable to thrive in a rigid hierarchy where managers are too strongly focused on their rank and title, rather than on their credibility.

Dave Ulrich, of the University of Michigan, talks about leadership as being the product of capability and credibility. In my view, it takes a potent cocktail of the forty identified qualities of leadership to achieve this.

A major problem in most organisations, is that managers are generally individuals who were capable of undertaking or managing certain tasks. This capability led to promotion and all of a sudden, an individual with talents relating to the manage-ment of tasks finds themselves in a position of managing people . . . a different challenge, more often than not requiring a different skill set and basket of qualities. Organisations need to consider employing individuals with leadership qualities to ultimately fill roles which do actually require a leader.

Remember, our companies are not machines, they are living organisms. To manage the former requires a passion for tools and technology, to manage the latter requires a passion for people.

Without a passion for people, I cannot see how anyone can be a leader. If you have a passion for people, you are more likely to be able to create a sense of community with aligned vision and values . . . an environment where empire-building and the

protection of one's turf is not
acceptable and where power
and information is readily
shared. In this type of
environment, leadership is
encouraged throughout the

Without a passion for people, I cannot see how anyone can be a leader.

organisation. Who actually leads at a given time is dependent on the situation, not rank or title.

The traditional management style and hierarchy has predominantly rewarded ability and short-term achievement of results. Where modern management has tried to imitate leadership, it is the areas of charisma, communication skills or vision building that they have inevitably focused on. The reason for this is that these are the attributes or qualities that managers think will transform them into leaders.

The focus on these elements of leadership has distracted us from some of the other very important qualities of leadership. Perhaps one of the most important is intelligence. Intelligence is to the leader what agility is to the gymnast, strength to the weightlifter and speed to the sprinter . . . it is the least often considered quality of leadership. The leaders of our organisations and companies of today and tomorrow need to have a deep and powerful intellect; a mind that is agile and flexible, able to shape and generate new ideas and opportunities.

The ability to think inductively is a prerequisite for a leader of an organisation or company, otherwise you will get locked into the cycle of identifying a problem, finding a solution and repeating the cycle.

Inductive thinking allows one solution to be so powerful as to address a wide range of problems, including those not yet identified.

Leaders have the intelligence to challenge conventional thinking, to develop possibilities not yet charted, to invent new opportunities, to think across traditional boundaries and to make unorthodox mental connections. It is the latter that often forms the basis of innovation.

What I am claiming, is that certain individuals can make a significant difference to the future of an organisation or company. These individuals are leaders who have the ability to shape the future, unlike the managers who all too often seem powerless recipients of their environment, which then shapes them and their organisation.

TWELVE | THE CURSE OF ASSUMPTION

Managers count seeds in the apple, while leaders
envision how many apples there are in one seed.

— Ian Percy

The business and management literature sometimes creaks under
the load of information on leadership. Leadership theories
abound and fads arise, only to fade away. Most of the writing on
leadership, however, is valuable and offers wisdom, perspective
and experience to shape the debate.

While the debate is intriguing, interesting and stimulating,
and some of the research fascinating, some of it curious, in the
end we are so often left with little real understanding of whether
leadership is present in our own organisation or not. The
introduction of The Whirlpool Effect™ is driven by a more
practical approach. It is something that can be applied to *your*
organisation or company.

It seeks to determine the level of connection between
management and employees, answering the most basic question
about leadership — if the senior executive has elected to lead,

have the employees elected to follow?

The Whirlpool Effect™ model further determines the balance across the four cornerstones of Purpose, Planning, Process and People. An imbalance can create a critical weakness, which may cause the organisation or company to stagnate, deteriorate slowly or rapidly lose control and collapse.

Furthermore, application of The Whirlpool Effect™ model can create an early-warning system to identify when the organisation or company is beginning to drift out of the placid water, and if it has, what level of danger it is exposed to.

The Whirlpool Effect™ concept and model is not a simple answer to a complex question. It is a pragmatic, conceptual and diagnostic tool that has a real-world application. I have not contemplated that it would be utilised on a stand-alone basis — the issue of leadership and its effects in an organisation or company are far too complex for that. It is an additional tool that managers can apply to assist them in developing a greater understanding of their own organisations.

Identifying management-employee disconnections and placing them in a context of danger can assist managers in gaining a clearer insight and help overcome one of the most insidious and dangerous diseases of modern management . . . the 'curse of assumption'.

Management often makes poorly judged assumptions about their organisations, these being the result of arrogance, ignorance or an unwillingness to confront reality. In the worst possible case, there is a combination of all of the above. These 'curses of assumption' usually occur as a result of management being remote from the consequences of both their actions and their decisions.

✿ THE YELLOW VIRUS . . . LESS COMMUNICABLE THAN I THOUGHT

IN MY FIRST MAJOR GENERAL MANAGEMENT ROLE, I FOUND myself heading an organisation of close to 1,500 employees.

I was determined to ensure open and frequent communication, especially as the organisation was moving through some reasonably significant change.

As part of my communication mix I wrote a newsletter. I selected canary yellow paper, a colour to be used only by me and only for the newsletter. In this way any employee who saw canary yellow amongst their papers or on a noticeboard would automatically know it was the newsletter and could then read it. The newsletter soon became known as the 'yellow virus'.

I personally wrote the newsletter, which was then photocopied, collated and distributed through the 'communication tree', basically a reflection of the organisation structure. As I moved around the organisation, however, it soon became apparent that large numbers of employees were not receiving a newsletter. I was disappointed and perplexed.

I dug a little deeper and found that the new approach to open communication was not shared in practice by many of the line managers. When they and I got together and discussed open communication, information sharing, breaking down traditional barriers, shifting and sharing power, I was met with smiling faces and nodding heads. But for some, the level of disclosure and openness of the communication was just too much, so they never passed the newsletters on to their reports. This was amazing, but not all that surprising, given management's propensity to control.

One day when I was talking to a union representative about communication and the difficulty I had in reaching frontline staff in any certain way, he suggested using the union communication process through the workplace delegates.

I did this by dividing the newsletters into two, one for the management communication tree and one for the union's communication process.

Suddenly the potency and communicability of the 'yellow virus' increased. The newsletter was now reaching almost all employees.

Had I not sought feedback about these newsletters as I moved about the organisation, I could have continued to communicate with wastebins and shredders, as line management attempted to short-circuit my communication agenda. I would have become a victim of the 'curse of assumption'.

Watch out, it is a real problem, I know, I have been caught out so many times.

The Whirlpool Effect™ model can assist in lifting the veil and identifying if assumptions you, as the senior executive, have made are mainly right or mainly wrong. Minimising or eliminating 'curses of assumption' is critically important to any manager. Because they are not remote from the consequence of management's actions and decisions, employees are usually very aware of these disconnections.

Management's unawareness of the disconnections will often lead to them communicating and acting inappropriately, often causing irrevocable harm to their credibility. Credibility is the heartbeat of leadership; I do not believe it is possible to lead without credibility. You can head an organisation, company, community or country without credibility, but if you cannot lead it, there will be no hope of that organisation, company, community or country reaching its potential. In any organisation the senior executive will only have the support, commitment and trust of their employees if the senior executive has credibility. Even the senior executive with limitless capability will be unable to make any achievement by themselves. They need their employees to align their talents, will and energy to create success.

> **Credibility is the heartbeat of leadership; I do not believe it is possible to lead without credibility.**

The head of any organisation or company who thinks they have real authority is misleading themselves. Authority is not conferred by rank, position or title; rather, it is conferred by employees who support their senior management. That support will only be strong and consistent if the senior executive has credibility.

❧ SIX VOTES COUNT FOR NOTHING

I REMEMBER ARRIVING FOR WORK THE FIRST DAY AS CHIEF executive of a large organisation of close to 4,000 employees.

I was anxious — no, make that vulnerable. Okay, make that terrified.

Why was I terrified? Well I had been appointed to the chief executive position by a board of directors of six individuals. On my first day at work, I had the vote of only six people out of almost 4,000 . . . and those six were not even there, being non-executive directors.

Believe me, employees do vote. They vote by coming to work, they vote by working when they come to work, they vote by 'going the extra mile'. As a chief executive, if you cannot build strong support amongst employees for the purpose, plans and process of your organisation or company, then you will fail to achieve potential.

Credibility takes time to develop and when you have it, remember this . . . credibility can be lost incredibly quickly.

Nonetheless it remains the platform for leadership. Credibility matters.

Application of The Whirlpool Effect™ model will give you a snapshot or broadbrush insight into your own credibility in your organisation or company. This is information you vitally need to know.

🌀 I BEAT YOU ONCE, THEREFORE I AM FASTER THAN YOU

WHEN I WAS AT SCHOOL I USED TO EXCEL IN WHAT WAS THEN the 100 yard dash (now the 100 metre sprint).

We had a trial to select the fastest athlete over 100 yards in each age group to determine who would represent the school at the inter-school athletic events. I won the trial and was selected. The boy who came second approached me to see if I would race him again, as it was a close finish and he believed that given another opportunity, he could beat me.

I was pleased to have won the trial and selection and

told him so. He pleaded with me, but I declined.

Whenever our paths crossed, which was often, he would challenge me to a race and I would decline again.

Soon he spread the word that I was scared to face his challenge and therefore I must have known he was faster than me. Doubt about my ability as the fastest over 100 yards in my age group spread . . . my credibility as an athlete plummeted.

I could not understand what was happening. I had beaten him over the past four years and again in the trial. I had not lost a race, so why should questions about my pace arise?

This story goes to the core of credibility. It is not about your confidence in your own ability, it is about the confidence of others.

I was so miserable about the whole issue, but I was not prepared to race him, because I had won the trial. However, one of my teachers approached me and told me that the issue needed to be resolved.

'You may know that you are the fastest, but now that there is doubt, you will need to prove it again,' he said.

'Why?' I asked.

'Because this is information you now need more than anyone else . . . you need to know, for your own credibility.'

To be frank, I still did not understand at the time. I felt pressured, but agreed to a further trial, which I won. The matter was laid to rest. Years later the significance of this event dawned on me.

Whenever I was asked why I would not meet the challenge of a new trial, I would merely say, 'Why should I, I am the fastest.' However, my actions were not consistent with my words. If I was so sure I was the fastest, why not prove it by rerunning the trial?

The reason I did not want to rerun the trial is that I was scared I would lose my position on the team. Deep down, my position was more important to me than whether I was truly the fastest. I did not want to know, even though I needed to know.

Managers are similar. They avoid developing an insight into their own credibility because they are scared. That is understandable. What is not understandable is that they put their organisation or company at risk because of their self-interest.

I am with Cheryl Breetwor who said, 'You can't be motivated by self-interest and expect to be a leader.'

To be a leader requires you to confront and deal with your own fears. You cannot do this unless you have insight and The Whirlpool Effect™ can assist in developing this insight.

The weather-related imagery used in The Whirlpool Effect™ is deliberate. Most people check the weather forecast at least once a day, often more than once. They like to know what the weather will be like so that they can choose the appropriate clothing and footwear, allow adequate time to reach a destination, plan an outing on the boat or a picnic. What they are doing is identifying if the weather is going to be a threat or an opportunity, so they can plan accordingly.

To be a leader requires you to confront and deal with your own fears.

If the forecast is for severe weather, people may rethink their plans and priorities. In the event of a weather crisis, for example very severe gales, a hurricane or tornado, they will focus almost exclusively on that until the danger has passed.

The Whirlpool Effect™ model can act as a weather forecast for an organisation, identifying the weather pattern and alerting the organisation or company to threatening or imminent danger. Managers need to constantly be assessing their position in the whirlpool, as the current has a natural tendency to flow towards danger, rather than away from it. Organisations or companies are the same. The natural tendency is towards poor performance and decline, rather than good performance or growth.

If a manager is aware that the organisation is in Zone Three, or more crucially in Zone Two, then postponing action for a further series of reviews, assessments and navel-gazing, would be most inappropriate. It is likely that inaction due to intense and unhelpful analysis and review is a contributing factor to the positioning in the first place. What is required is leadership and action.

Have you noticed when travelling by airplane that the mood of the passengers is different when the weather is clear and cloudless, compared to when there are high winds, driving rain and no visibility? The weather is an important factor for an airplane and its safe journey. It is no different for an organisation or company, except that management is often oblivious to the fact that the company is passing through troubled water, on the way to the whirlpool.

This is largely due to management's 'blindspot' for the intangibles. Their unhealthy, single-minded focus on measuring 'lagging' tangible indicators obscures the real picture. The Whirlpool Effect™ model assists in developing an understanding of the critical intangibles, which in reality drive the tangible measures.

The need for everything to be distilled to a tangible element, preferably a set of numbers in a spreadsheet, is at the core of the problem with modern management. They are worshipping at the wrong altar — the lap-top computer.

> It may appear more than a little unfair to describe modern management as 'fit to manage, but unfit to lead', but in general, the label fits.

It is the 'neck-top' computer that should be the altar. The 'neck-top' computer is able to outperform a lap-top computer in critical areas of judgment, instinct, sense of timing and anticipation. When was the last time a lap-top computer inspired you to commit to a purpose with your heart and soul? Never.

It may appear more than a little unfair to describe modern management as 'fit to manage, but unfit to lead', but in general, the label fits. Management is strong on rhetoric but is in reality a conformist 'society' where challenge to the status quo and the status of management is definitely discouraged. The management 'establishment' is the single most significant impediment to organisations and companies reaching their potential.

Too much of modern management is focused on running their own private agenda, be it one of self-interest, pay-back, unfulfilled ambition or envy. They usually do this with someone else's money — in many cases, alarmingly, with public money. The credibility of management is low and needs to be restored. The first step is self-awareness and an understanding that to be an exceptional manager

> Too much of modern management is focused on running their own private agenda, be it one of self-interest, pay-back, unfulfilled ambition or envy.

is extraordinarily difficult. It requires a magical blend of the left brain and the right brain, of rational thought and a passionate perspective, the ability to think deductively as well as inductively, to have rigour and discipline as well as flexibility and experimentation. It requires education and experience, form as well as substance . . . it requires character and courage.

> **Our managers need to be armed with the capabilities of courage, vision, integrity and instinct, not just with the ability to read balance sheets and undertake performance appraisals.**

It is time to review the education of management. There needs to be a greater emphasis on process over content and we must teach what is important, not what we are comfortable teaching. Our managers need to be armed with the capacities of courage, vision, integrity and instinct, not just with the ability to read balance sheets and undertake performance appraisals.

Management is much more about understanding, influencing and shaping human behaviour and interactions than about performing technical tasks. Modern management's approach and attitude stifles and suffocates leadership, rather than stimulating and encouraging it. Organisations and companies, schools and universities, communities and countries, need to identify those boys and girls, men and women, with the uncommon but important gifts of leadership, the 'inner circle qualities of leadership'. Once identified they need the appropriate education and experience to play out their role in life . . . as leaders.

I have no expectation that we should discard all of our modern management in favour of leaders. Firstly, there would not be enough leaders to replace them, and secondly, there is a role for the exceptional manager who will never be the exceptional leader . . . but it is not the leadership role, as so often occurs.

> **Those who have succeeded as leaders are left with a lifelong responsibility to assist with the development of the next generation of leaders.**

Perhaps what we need more than anything is the phenomenon described by Craig Hickman — an individual with the 'mind of a manager and the soul of a leader'.

Even for those blessed with a blend of the natural qualities of leadership, leadership itself is a continuous process of learning. As with sport, the best way to learn is by practising. No one becomes a gifted artist or sporting star just by reading the theory.

Those who have succeeded as leaders are left with a lifelong responsibility to assist with the development of the next generation of leaders. To ignore this responsibility would call their role of a leader into question.

It has been my privilege to share The Whirlpool Effect™ and my perspectives on leadership with you. I have been absorbed by human behaviour in organisations and companies for two decades now, with an interest in how leadership can help an organisation or company reach its potential. I do not wish to be offensive to modern management, but I believe they need a call to action. Their position, status and rewards are often unmatched by performance and this is not right.

Whether you agree with what you have read or whether you do not, is not what is important. What is important is that you are stimulated to think about the critical issues of management and leadership and why the traditional style of management has failed us.

I am left in no doubt about the powerful impact great leadership has on the ability of an organisation or company to reach its potential. This book is about my views and thoughts on leadership, shaped by reading, thinking, experience and the exchange of ideas. It is not about me. In my own management career I have made blunders but I have always tried to learn from them and have come to value having the 'test first and the lesson afterwards'.

Isaac Newton once said, 'If I have seen further it is because I stood on the shoulders of giants.' I have been fortunate to be involved in a number of successful ventures when I was in the role of a senior executive. My own experience is that the successes I have been involved with are simply the result of 'standing on the shoulders of giants' — the people I worked for and the people I worked with. You may notice that there is no mention of the people who worked *for* me. If there is anything at all to be learned from me, it is that no matter what position I held, I never ever, ever, thought of anyone working for me . . . only *with* me, and me with them.

I started my working life as a medical doctor and serendipity catapulted me into positions where I needed to function as a leader. I always put my heart and soul into those roles but I am not in a position to assess my performance. I am, however, in a position to thank all those employees who lent me their support, often in difficult situations. I have the greatest respect and affection for them — they are the real heroes.

PART 7

THE WHIRLPOOL EFFECT™
SURVEY

THE WHIRLPOOL EFFECT™
SURVEY

For each of the following 24 Lines of Leadership, please place a cross on the line at the level which best indicates how you feel about the Line of Leadership in relation to your company or organisation. Note that 0 is the lowest score possible and 10 is the highest score that may be given.

For example:

LINE OF LEADERSHIP: CLARITY OF PURPOSE

If you felt that your company or organisation had no clarity of purpose at all, you would indicate your feelings by placing a cross on level 0.

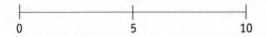

```
0              5              10
```

Conversely, if you felt that your company or organisation had absolute clarity of purpose, you would indicate your feelings by placing a cross on Level 10.

However, if you felt that the clarity of purpose for your company or organisation was somewhere in between, you would indicate your feelings by placing a cross on the line at the level which best represents your perception.

Certain lines of leadership call for an assessment of the depth of, the level of, the degree of, the degree of which. In all of these cases 0 still indicates the lowest assessment and 10 the highest.

CORNERSTONES AND LINES OF LEADERSHIP

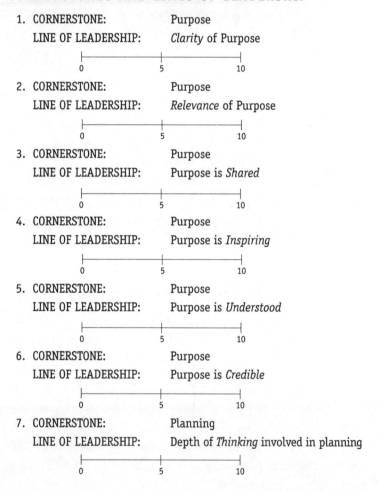

1. CORNERSTONE: Purpose
   LINE OF LEADERSHIP: *Clarity* of Purpose

   |—————————————|—————————————|
   0   5   10

2. CORNERSTONE: Purpose
   LINE OF LEADERSHIP: *Relevance* of Purpose

   |—————————————|—————————————|
   0   5   10

3. CORNERSTONE: Purpose
   LINE OF LEADERSHIP: Purpose is *Shared*

   |—————————————|—————————————|
   0   5   10

4. CORNERSTONE: Purpose
   LINE OF LEADERSHIP: Purpose is *Inspiring*

   |—————————————|—————————————|
   0   5   10

5. CORNERSTONE: Purpose
   LINE OF LEADERSHIP: Purpose is *Understood*

   |—————————————|—————————————|
   0   5   10

6. CORNERSTONE: Purpose
   LINE OF LEADERSHIP: Purpose is *Credible*

   |—————————————|—————————————|
   0   5   10

7. CORNERSTONE: Planning
   LINE OF LEADERSHIP: Depth of *Thinking* involved in planning

   |—————————————|—————————————|
   0   5   10

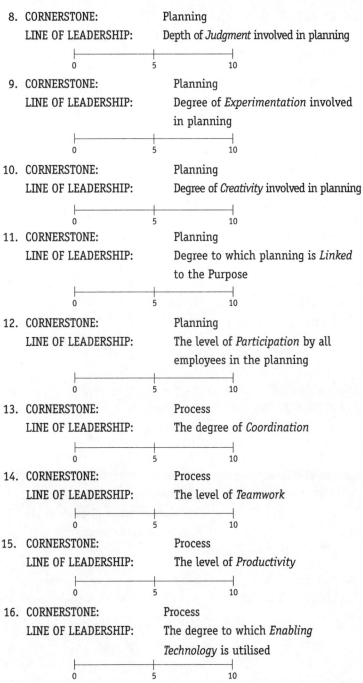

8. CORNERSTONE: Planning
   LINE OF LEADERSHIP: Depth of *Judgment* involved in planning

   |———————————|———————————|
   0   5   10

9. CORNERSTONE: Planning
   LINE OF LEADERSHIP: Degree of *Experimentation* involved
                           in planning

   |———————————|———————————|
   0   5   10

10. CORNERSTONE: Planning
    LINE OF LEADERSHIP: Degree of *Creativity* involved in planning

   |———————————|———————————|
   0   5   10

11. CORNERSTONE: Planning
    LINE OF LEADERSHIP: Degree to which planning is *Linked*
                           to the Purpose

   |———————————|———————————|
   0   5   10

12. CORNERSTONE: Planning
    LINE OF LEADERSHIP: The level of *Participation* by all
                           employees in the planning

   |———————————|———————————|
   0   5   10

13. CORNERSTONE: Process
    LINE OF LEADERSHIP: The degree of *Coordination*

   |———————————|———————————|
   0   5   10

14. CORNERSTONE: Process
    LINE OF LEADERSHIP: The level of *Teamwork*

   |———————————|———————————|
   0   5   10

15. CORNERSTONE: Process
    LINE OF LEADERSHIP: The level of *Productivity*

   |———————————|———————————|
   0   5   10

16. CORNERSTONE: Process
    LINE OF LEADERSHIP: The degree to which *Enabling
                           Technology* is utilised

   |———————————|———————————|
   0   5   10

17. CORNERSTONE: Process
    LINE OF LEADERSHIP: The level of *Quality*

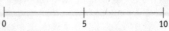

   0   5   10

18. CORNERSTONE: Process
    LINE OF LEADERSHIP: The degree to which *Values* are shared
    and clear

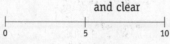

   0   5   10

19. CORNERSTONE: People
    LINE OF LEADERSHIP: The level of *Empowerment*

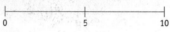

   0   5   10

20. CORNERSTONE: People
    LINE OF LEADERSHIP: The level of *Trust*

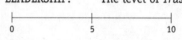

   0   5   10

21. CORNERSTONE: People
    LINE OF LEADERSHIP: The degree to which all employees are
    treated with *Dignity*

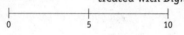

   0   5   10

22. CORNERSTONE: People
    LINE OF LEADERSHIP: The degree to which *Preventative
    Recruitment* is practised

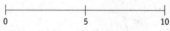

   0   5   10

23. CORNERSTONE: People
    LINE OF LEADERSHIP: The degree to which principles and
    mechanisms are in place to ensure
    employees are *Retained*

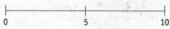

   0   5   10

24. CORNERSTONE: People
    LINE OF LEADERSHIP: The degree to which 'well-poisoners' are
    Released

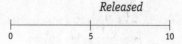

   0   5   10